MORI [illegible] E

MORE WAYS THAN ONE

Evangelism in the Post-Modern World

J.John
Barry Woodward
Mark Greenwood
Joseph Boot
Paul McGee
Anthony Delaney
Dave Edwards
David McDougall
Greg Downes
Roy Todd
Don Egan
Mark Ritchie
Steve Legg
Ian Wilson
Andy Economides

Authentic

MILTON KEYNES • COLORADO SPRINGS • HYDERABAD

15 14 13 12 11 10 09 8 7 6 5 4 3 2 1

First published 2009 by Authentic Media
9 Holdom Avenue, Bletchley, Milton Keynes, MK1 1QR, UK
1820 Jet Stream Drive, Colorado Springs, CO 80921, USA
Medchal Road, Jeedimetla Village, Secunderabad 500 055, A.P., India
www.loveauthentic.com
Authentic Media is a division of Biblica UK, previously IBS-STL UK. Biblica UK is limited by guarantee, with its registered office at Kingstown Broadway, Carlisle, Cumbria, CA3 0HA. Registered in England & Wales No. 1216232. Registered charity in England & Wales No. 270162 and Scotland No. SCO40064.

British Library Cataloguing in Publication Data
A catalogue record for this book is available from the British Library

ISBN-13: 978-1-86024-722-4

Cover Design by Chris Jones
Print Management by Adare
Printed in Great Britain by J.F. Print, Sparkford

We dedicate our book to the
Revd Dr Michael Green.

You are an apostle, prophet, evangelist,
pastor and teacher.

You have truly embraced 'more ways than one'.
You are an inspiration to us.

Thank you.

Happy 80th birthday!

Contents

Contributors' Biographies

Joseph Boot

Joe Boot is an apologist, educator, author and the senior pastor of Westminster Chapel, Toronto. He served with Ravi Zacharias for seven years as an apologist in the UK and Canada, working for five years as Canadian director of RZIM. He has spoken in twenty-five countries in universities, seminaries, churches, conferences and has publicly debated with leading atheists in North American universities.

His apologetic works have been published in Europe and in North America. Including *Searching for Truth, Why I Still Believe* and his latest volume, *How Then Shall We Answer.*

Joe lives near Toronto with his wife Jenny and their three children Naomi, Hannah and Isaac.

For more information visit: www.westminsterchapel.ca

Anthony Delaney

Anthony Delaney was a police officer in Manchester for twelve years before being called into ordained Anglican ministry. He served in various churches in the south of

England. In September 2008 he returned to his roots in Manchester, and now leads Ivy Manchester, a growing, vibrant church in Didsbury. Married to Zoe, he has three children.

For more information visit:www.anthonydelaney.com

Greg Downes

After studying for a degree in Social Policy and Administration, Greg did a PGCE in Religious Education and taught RE at a school in London.

He later studied theology at Oxford and then was ordained in the Church of England. Since then Greg has been a curate in High Wycombe, Senior Chaplain of HMP & YOI Ashfield near Bristol, Tutor in Evangelism at the London School of Theology and a chaplain at Oxford University. He is now the Principal of the Watford School of Leadership, which exists to train ordinary Christians to become transformational leaders in the world. For more information visit www.wsol.org.uk.

Andy Economides

Revd Andy Economides is an international evangelist. He is the founding director of Soteria Trust, which shares the Good News, disciples, teaches and equips. The Soteria College in Nigeria offers education for job opportunities and disciples young people.

While Andy was studying engineering in London he met J.John and brought him to Christ and discipled him. Discipleship has always been at the forefront of Andy's life and work. He has also written several books.

For more information visit: www.soteriatrust.org.uk

David Edwards

David Edwards worked for seven years as assistant and worship leader with J.John. Since that time he has led worship at many of J.John's evangelistic missions.

David is now on staff as Worship Co-ordinator at St Andrew's Church in Cullompton, Devon. He also travels further afield to speak and to lead worship.

He is married to Nikki. They have four children: Sam, Emily, Josh and Daniel.

For more information visit: www.asaphworship.co.uk

Don Egan

Don Egan is a Christian speaker, writer and evangelist. Over the last twenty years, Don has been used in bringing God's healing power to many in Africa and the UK.

Don served as an Anglican minister for eleven years, in two parishes – first in Manchester and then in Stowmarket, Suffolk.

In 1994 he founded the RSVP Trust as he began a series of missions in the Philippines, Uganda, Rwanda, Tanzania, Kenya and Nigeria, as well as continuing to travel throughout the UK.

In 1997 Don witnessed amazing healing miracles in his meetings in Rwanda – a woman who had been blind for twelve years began to see. In other meetings, the blind saw, the lame walked and the deaf heard.

In the UK too, healing regularly occurs when Don speaks. Blind people recover their sight, and joints and spines are healed of severe pain. A woman who had been unable to have children gave birth to a beautiful daughter. A woman who had been registered blind for twenty-five years suddenly recovered her sight.

Don is the author of several books and is married to Hazel.

For more information visit: www.rsvptrust.co.uk

Mark Greenwood

Mark Greenwood lives in Warwickshire with his wife Emma and their two children, Robin and Nathalie. He has been in full-time preaching evangelism for twenty years.

Mark uses humour and thought-provoking chat to unpack the gospel for unbelievers, often being compared to Peter Kay. As an evangelist Mark believes his gift from God is something he should not only use but develop and sharpen constantly. To do this Mark has done extensive personal study and research into humour and how it can be best used to present the gospel. Alongside this Mark performs in some secular stand-up shows with full-time secular comedians.

For more information visit: www.fortythreetrust.com

J.John

J.John, a Greek-Cypriot by birth, lives in Chorleywood, Hertfordshire in England. He is married to Killy and they have three sons – Michael, Simeon and Benjamin.

J.John is regarded as a creative speaker with an appeal that transcends gender, age, race, culture and occupation. His much-loved art of storytelling helps people to discover spiritual meaning in a way that makes sense of everyday life.

To date, he has completed thousands of speaking engagements at conferences, towns, cities and universities in fifty-four countries on six continents.

For more information visit: www.philotrust.com

Steve Legg

Steve Legg is a creative evangelist from West Sussex in England. For twenty years he has used a mix of illusion, comedy and escapology to communicate the gospel, and this has taken him across the length and breadth of the UK and to twenty other countries around the world.

In recent years Steve has developed a Christmas cartoon called *It's a Boy!* and has written thirteen books. He is also the managing editor and publisher of *Sorted* magazine, an innovative publication for men which the *Daily Telegraph* has called 'the lad's mag with morals'. He is married to Rebekah and they have six children.

For more information visit: www.breakout.org.uk and www.sorted-magazine.com

David McDougall

David McDougall is an Anglican church planter living in Sunbury, Middlesex. He is married to Kim with three teenagers – Nicol, Jamie and Arran.

David is known for his enthusiasm and unstoppable love for Jesus. He travels widely, believing that mission needs to be at 'home and away'. He has been in Anglican ministry for twenty-one years. He is on the English Board for 'Watoto', a Christian project based at Kampala Pentecostal Church which is presently housing, educating and looking after 1,800 Ugandan orphans.

At present he lives in Sunbury, where, with a team he has planted an Anglican church which has grown from a congregation of 50 to 300 in 6 years.

For more information visit: www.st-saviours-sunbury.org.uk

Paul McGee

Paul McGee is a Christian speaker and the author of the best-selling book *SUMO* (*Shut Up, Move On*). He has spoken in thirty countries, running seminars and master-classes and speaking at conferences.

Paul spends 90 per cent of his time communicating godly principles and kingdom values to secular organizations – speaking God's truths and heart for people, but without using overt Christian language. His material addresses issues related to Leadership, Succeeding through change, Building better relationships, Attitude, Motivation and Stress. The other 10 per cent of his time is spent working with churches and Christian organizations in the UK and around the world.

To see a five-minute clip of Paul speaking, please go to: www.TheSumoGuy.com/media.php

For more information visit: www.TheSumoGuy.com

Mark Ritchie

Mark left Musselburgh, Scotland in 1987 to spend three years at Mattersey Hall Bible College. For over twelve years he has communicated the gospel to thousands at conferences, football stadiums and various venues across the UK and around the world. Currently based in Nottingham with his wife Tamzin, his son Jordan and daughter Keziah, Mark's desire is to communicate the gospel of Jesus Christ in a way which is creative, innovative and relevant to those who have not yet been impacted by the Good News of Jesus Christ.

Mark is currently touring with his evangelistic one-man theatre show. The show mixes his unique blend of humour with the gospel message. His stories are interlaced with humour and interaction that motivate people in their personal, spiritual and working lives.

For more information visit: www.73rdtrust.com

Roy Todd

Roy Todd is a UK-based evangelist who travels internationally, communicating the Good News of Jesus Christ and praying for people to experience his healing in their lives.

Many people have become Christians at events led by Roy, and numerous others believe they have been miraculously healed from conditions such as deafness, blindness, cancer and much more.

For more information visit: www.roytodd.org

Ian Wilson

Ian Wilson is a dentist and an evangelist. He and his wife Andie moved out to Tanzania in 2002 in response to God's call on their lives. They now have four children – Jake, Imani, Neema and Maisha. They belong to Revelation Church, Chichester and are part of the leadership team of Bridge2Aid, a UK-registered dental/ community development charity.

During their time in Tanzania they have seen the need to re-examine mission in a new cultural setting and to explore with others what authentic mission looks like in a cross-cultural context.

For more information visit: www.bridge2aid.org

Barry Woodward

Barry Woodward grew up in Greater Manchester, England. At the age of 16 he left school without any qualifications and was drawn into the drug scene, experimenting with cannabis, amphetamines and LSD. This led to a heroin addiction and life as a drugs supplier.

For fourteen years he was totally dependent on drugs, during which time he spent a number of terms in prison. Miraculously, his life turned around completely following an amazing sequence of supernatural encounters.

Barry is now an evangelist and travels throughout the United Kingdom communicating the Good News of Christianity, using vivid storytelling and humour. He is the founder of Proclaim Trust. He is also the author of the best-selling book, *Once an Addict*.

For more information visit: www.proclaimtrust.org

Foreword

I am delighted to commend this unusual volume on evangelism. Evangelism itself is none too common in the West – we have much to learn from Africa, South America and Southeast Asia – but when it happens these days, it is normally through preaching in church or running an Alpha course. There seems to be a distinct lack of imagination and spontaneity among us. And that is sad, both because Scripture is so rich in suggestions about evangelism, and because the church through the centuries has been highly innovative. It would be tragic if, in this pluralist and post-Christian society, which covers much of Europe and is invading North America, we succumbed to a one-track and often boring way of presenting the greatest news the world has ever heard. This book is a delightful pointer to a whole variety of ways of spreading the gospel.

It is inevitably uneven, as all such books with corporate authorship must be, but I challenge anyone who has a heart for evangelism to read this book without gaining lots of good ideas. It is fresh and remarkably comprehensive.

One of the things that pleases me most about the book is that it comes from a circle of younger evangelists, whom J.John has been nurturing for some time. He is arguably the best evangelistic preacher in Britain today. But rather than operating like a prima donna, he regularly takes younger colleagues with him on evangelistic forays. Like the apostle Paul, he pours himself into equipping others, and takes more delight in their successes than his own. He reminds me of Paul's words, 'the things you have heard me say in the presence of many witnesses entrust to reliable men who will also be qualified to teach others' (2 Tim. 2:2 NIV). The reliable men you will find in this volume. They are qualified to teach us how to do evangelism better, and to realize that there are indeed *more ways than one*. J.John's aim has been not to produce clones of himself, of course, but to sharpen and develop the God-given talents this varied group of evangelists possesses. This book is in a very real sense the fruit of his labours, as well as theirs.

It has long been recognized among New Testament scholars that the Fourth Gospel emerged not from one man alone, but from a 'Johannine circle', alluded to in John 21:24. But there are all too few modern examples of gifted leaders doing the same thing. They pour themselves out exhaustively in the pastoring, authorship or evangelistic work in which they excel, but they do not leave behind them a group of men and women whom they have nurtured and whose skills they have honed. J.John has chosen a better path. He follows the example of his apostolic namesake. And the result of this group's labours, and the sharing of their experience in spreading the gospel, can be a beacon of light to us all.

Revd Dr Michael Green,
Oxford, England

Preface

For fifteen years Andy Economides and I have been meeting annually with a group of evangelists. We call these gatherings '*Sovrakon*' (the Greek word for 'pants', or to our US readers, 'underwear') to remind us of who we are and bring us down to earth!

The banter at our meetings is always engaging, at times tearful and frequently humorous. The combined creativity and synergy is quite volcanic!

It was at one of our meals that someone suggested that we each write a chapter in our area of expertise and offer it as a combined volume. So here is our offering, with our breadcrumbs of wisdom which we have picked up along the way.

I would like to acknowledge and thank Greg Downes who edited all the chapters and refined them. Greg you are both a theologian and an evangelist and you wisely and skilfully shaped the book – THANK YOU.

My friends and I hope and pray that as you read through our book, you will agree that there are 'more ways than one' and that 'none of us have got it together, but together we have got it'!

J.John

Chapter 1

How to Communicate Effectively
Evangelism through preaching

J.John

> 'Where shall I begin, please your majesty?' she asked.
> 'Begin at the beginning,' the king said very gravely, 'and go on till you come to the end: then stop.'
>
> Lewis Carroll,
> *Alice's Adventures in Wonderland* (1865)

One chapter on evangelistic preaching – wherever do I begin? For some in the church, our calling and gifting is to proclaim, preach and teach.

The Greek word for 'proclaim', *keruss*, which is used sixty times in the New Testament, literally means 'to make a public announcement from a king'. This reminds us that our message is from God, who is the King of all, and therefore we should not be timid in our speaking.

The Greek word for 'preach', *euaggelizo*, from which we get the English word 'evangelize', is used fifty times in the New Testament. It is usually translated 'preach the gospel' or 'preach good news'. This reminds us that our message, especially to the unchurched, has to be *good* news.

G.K. Chesterton said: 'It's a sin to present the Gospel – the greatest story ever told – in a dull, uninspired, joyless and humourless manner.'

The apostle Paul's words to Timothy, 'do the work of an evangelist' (2 Tim. 4:5 NIV), have often been misinterpreted as meaning, 'Timothy, you're a pastor. Don't be a pastor any more. Do the work of an evangelist.' I think the apostle Paul meant: 'Timothy, you're a pastor; do it as if you were an evangelist.' To others he might have said: You're a teacher; do it as if you were an evangelist. You're a secretary; do it as if you were an evangelist. You're a cleaner; do it as if you were an evangelist. I want to say to preachers: preach as if you were an evangelist. It is a mind-set.

As part of a survey,[1] 1,000 churches were asked the question: 'In the last ten years have you taught and equipped your church how to evangelize?' Only 36 churches (3.6 per cent) answered 'yes'. The church is about three things: Worship, Well-being and Witness. However, the reality is that the church spends at least 90 per cent of its time on Worship and Well-being and *only* 10 per cent on Witness. There is an imbalance. Why not allocate 33 per cent to each?

Effective preaching comes from who you are

Before I offer some tips for how to sharpen your evangelistic edge when preaching, I want to stress that effective evangelistic preaching cannot be separated from the life of the preacher. Without a heart for evangelism, whatever I might try to teach preachers about evangelistic preaching, it would simply be clinical. Without a passion for lost people, our evangelistic preaching will not be effective. As my friend Dr

Michael Green says, there is no shortcut to having 'fire in our belly'.

Imagine my wife and I and our three sons decide to go to the forest, have a barbecue and play games. When it is time to go home, once we have packed everything up, we discover that only one son, Benjamin, is still with us. The other two, Simeon and Michael, are lost. We search for them in the forest and after a while we find Simeon. We can't find Michael.

Would we say, 'Oh, never mind. Let's just go home. At least we've got two of our sons'? No, of course not. We would search for Michael until we found him alive or dead. This is the kind of analogy that is used in Scripture to inspire us in our search for those who are lost and do not know Jesus.

A missionary is not someone who crosses the seas. A missionary is someone who sees the cross. That is why the apostle Paul said, 'the love of Christ compels us' (2 Cor. 5:14 NKJV). This love must come from the heart. If, as an individual, a preacher does not have a passion to seek and save the lost, then there is very little anyone can teach them about evangelistic preaching. They can learn some techniques, but in reality it is not going to do very much. We have got to revisit the cross and be empowered by God's Holy Spirit, because it is the love of Christ that compels us.

We need to allow God to use us as links in a chain. Sometimes people assume that every time I speak to an unbeliever about Christ they end up becoming a Christian. Often we get to share the love of God with someone but don't see the end result.

Recently I had a meeting in central London. Not wanting to be late, I set off in good time. I arrived an hour early, so I decided to get a cup of coffee. As I was walking through the shopping centre I saw a man cleaning shoes, and I thought I would get mine cleaned. Looking down and realizing my shoes were already clean, I was having second thoughts when I felt God prompt me to go ahead. Discovering it would cost £4, I hesitated once again, but God was still urging me on.

Sitting down on the chair, I asked the man cleaning shoes, 'Why do you look so sad?'

He said, 'How do you know I am sad?'

I said, 'I can see it in your eyes.'

He responded, 'I have cleaned many people's shoes. Hundreds. You are the first person who has ever said that to me.'

He started crying, so I asked him to tell me what it was about his story that made him sad. He spent the next twenty-five minutes telling me his story. When he had finished, I prayed with him and I gave him a book I had with me explaining the gospel, and then I dashed off to make my meeting. This man wasn't ready to become a Christian, but I trust that this positive encounter with a Christian who cared and listened will make him open to the Good News in the future.

After my meeting, feeling hungry, I decided to have a quick bite to eat before getting the train. I walked into a café and bought a sandwich, but I couldn't find anywhere to sit because all the tables were taken. I saw a table with only one man sitting at it, so I asked him if he would mind if I joined him.

'Oh no, that's fine,' he said and we exchanged a few pleasantries.

A thought came to my mind: *Ask him if he is married*. I thought that was an unusual thought, and wondered if the Holy Spirit had prompted it, so I asked him, 'Are you married?'

He replied, 'I can't believe you have asked me that question! I've been engaged to the same woman for seven years and I just can't get my act together to marry her.'

I explained a few things to him about relationships, commitment and marriage and said I would love to send him a book on marriage. I offered him my business card and asked him to email me if he wanted the book. By the time I got back to my office an hour later, he had already emailed me. He wrote: 'This has been one of the most intriguing conversations I have had in a long time. Yes, please, send me the book.' Both he and his fiancée read the book.

I tell these stories to make the point that, unless conversations like these are the normal practice of our daily lives, we are not going to be passionate or ultimately effective when we undertake to preach evangelistically.

That said, what tips would I offer the communicator who wishes to preach evangelistically?

Be yourself

'To thine own self be true' – advice from Shakespeare as relevant today as ever. I think this is so important. *Be yourself* – because no one else is qualified to do it! Don't try to be like someone else. I think the Lord would say to many of us, 'Why aren't you more like you?' There is a liberating freedom in being yourself. I have heard many preachers over the years and have learnt a lot about communication, but I have always endeavoured to be *me*. People need to know that 'what they see is what they get' and that we are the same on the stage as we are off the stage. We are not taking on a different persona when we preach. We can and should be relaxed and confident in who we are.

In Matthew 13, Jesus quoted Isaiah 6:9–10. He repeated the words 'seeing', 'hearing' and 'understanding' (or 'eyes', 'ears' and 'minds') four times. It is not accidental that on each occasion he says 'see' as well as 'hear'. It has a natural as well as a spiritual significance. We imagine that what we say is all-important, but we are mistaken. People hear our words but they see our body language. They notice how close we stand to people or how far away. Sometimes one distance is appropriate, sometimes another. When he was preaching to a large crowd on the seashore, Jesus – knowing they needed to see him – got into a boat that was pushed a little distance offshore. He sat, as other teachers did, because in those days sitting communicated authority. When we go up into a high pulpit, six feet above contradiction, it says something. Sometimes this is good, sometimes it is not.

The Gospels often describe the body language of Jesus: he stretched out his hand and touched a leper; he showed surprise at the Roman officer; he touched the eyes of the blind; his heart was filled with compassion; he took the five loaves and two fishes, looked up to heaven and gave thanks. When they brought to him the woman taken in adultery, they made her stand before them, but he bent over and wrote on the ground with his finger; he straightened up and spoke to them about throwing the first stone; he bent over again and wrote on the ground, and with only the woman still standing, he straightened up and asked her, 'Where are they?'

Jesus' body language spoke volumes. He turned his back on Peter; he placed his hands on the children; he wept at the grave of Lazarus.

Be prayerful

The Bible emphasizes *hearing* as well as *speaking*. We often have an urge and even a *need* to speak. Some of us speak because we are full and others of us speak because we are empty. When our need to speak is more important to us than other people's need to hear, there is a problem. We don't preach because we *want* to say something. We preach because we *have* something to say.

E. M. Bounds wrote: 'The character of our praying will determine the character of our preaching. Light praying makes light preaching.'

I think many preachers have got so many irons in the fire that they have put the fire out! What we need to do is to take some irons out of the fire and stoke it up. Someone once said, 'If our output exceeds our input, then our upkeep will be our downfall.'

That is why it is vital that we prepare *ourselves* as well as our sermons. It is essential that what we do *for God*, we do *with God*. Otherwise *the work of the Lord* becomes more important than *the Lord of the work* and we preach and teach in our own strength. It is good to be reminded that 'Unless the Lord builds the house, the labourers labour in vain.'

Søren Kierkegaard said: 'A preacher prayed and at first he thought prayer was talking. But he became more and more quiet until in the end he realized that prayer was listening.'

As the Psalmist wrote: 'Be still and I know that I am God.' Let us not be afraid to *retreat to advance*. We need to keep the reservoir full.

John Wesley (1703–91) wrote: 'Give me one hundred preachers who fear nothing but sin and desire nothing but God, and I care not a straw whether they be clergy or laity; such alone will shake the gates of hell and set up the kingdom of heaven on Earth. God does nothing, but in answer to prayer.'

We need God's anointing, which mediates his power and his presence, in order to be effective communicators of the Good News of Jesus Christ.

Be clear

What have I learnt from preaching evangelistically for thirty years? The art of effective communication involves three things:

1. Tell them what you are going to tell them.
2. Tell them.
3. Tell them what you told them.

One factor that needs to be in place to ensure maximum clarity is effective preparation. Many people who hear me preach totally unscripted assume that when I do that, I simply walk on the stage and make it up! On the contrary, speaking in a way that seems extempore requires even more preparation than speaking from a script. A former Archbishop of Canterbury, Robert Runcie, used to call such speaking 'calculated spontaneity'. Whenever I give a new talk, I always write out the text completely and ask my wife and various friends to read it through and critique it. It is a fascinating exercise. Sometimes I think we could all do a lot more of that, so that when we get up and preach, we can preach with more confidence, with more credibility and with clarity.

Another of the major problems in communicating clearly is in making ourselves understood. There is a placard frequently seen on office walls, which reads:

> I know you believe you understand what you think I said, but I'm not sure you realize that what you heard is not what I meant.

Often our attempts at communicating are distorted by misunderstanding. We speak out of our set of assumptions and our hearers listen through their own grid of past experience, misinformation and prejudice.

Communication experts have concluded that when we speak there are actually six messages that can come through:

1. What you mean to say.
2. What you actually say.
3. What a person hears.
4. What a person thinks they hear.
5. What a person says about what they think we said.
6. What we think the person said about what we said!

So it is essential that when we preach and speak, we endeavour to communicate in such a way that people understand what we are saying.

I heard the story of one man who pleaded with his pastor for opportunities to preach. But he was a bad communicator and his minister was understandably cautious.

He said to his pastor, 'Woe to me, if I do not preach the gospel!'

The pastor wisely replied, 'And woe to the poor congregation if you do!'

The people to whom we are communicating are of primary importance. I believe the best way to *be clear* is to *be simple*. Jesus taught profound truths in very simple ways, and many of us today do the opposite. We teach simple truths in profound ways and confuse people!

We need to preach *simply* without being *simplistic*. Don't be afraid to preach simply. I am always asking myself, 'Is there a simpler way to say it?'

I can testify from years of experience that the simpler I am, the more I connect with people, and consequently the response and fruit is greater.

Simple does not mean shallow; simple does not mean superficial. The Christian message is very simple. But Satan loves to complicate it. And sometimes Satan doesn't have to complicate it – we do it for him!

It is a misconception that you need to use theological jargon to teach theology. I love to teach theology at a very simple level, without using theological terms and without people knowing that I am teaching them theology.

Today people talk in *pictorial* terms to express inner *psychological* issues: 'I am ready to throw in the towel'; 'I'm at the end of my tether'; 'I am just a bundle of nerves'; 'I'm falling apart'; 'I'm at my wits' end'; 'I feel like resigning from the human race'. They do not say, 'I'm experiencing profound epistemological *angst*.' I know ministers who speak in an unknown tongue every week, and they aren't even charismatics! Our preaching of the message must be simple. We must work out ways of expressing profound theology pictorially in the language of the street.

One Easter Sunday I preached at Hillsong Church in London. My message was: 'Christianity is about forgiveness from the past, new life today and a hope for the future. If you want to have this offer, then you have to go via King's Cross.' That was my whole message. My teaching backed up that statement, and 269 people made a first-time commitment to Jesus Christ.

The apostle Paul wrote in 1 Corinthians 2:1–5 (NLT):

> When I first came to you . . . I didn't use lofty words and impressive wisdom to tell you God's secret plan . . . my message and my preaching were very plain. Rather than using clever and persuasive speeches, I relied only on the power of the Holy Spirit. I did this so you would trust not in human wisdom but in the power of God.

If the truths being preached cannot be understood with the worldview of our hearers, then we will make no sense at all. I read of a story about a Japanese convert from Shintoism who, having heard an explanation of the Trinity, said, 'Most High Person of Honourable Father, him I understand. Honourable Son, him also I understand. But please tell me who is that Honourable Bird?' The idea of the dove as a symbol of the Holy Spirit was incomprehensible to him. If we don't preach with clarity, it can lead to a distorted and confused version of the gospel.

This is what happened with the seed that fell on shallow ground. The hearers accepted a gospel that they thought promised them a prosperous and easy life. When trouble and persecution arose, they gave up following Christ.

When the apostle Paul preached in Antioch, he used many references to the Old Testament because his hearers were Jews and they knew the Scriptures (see Acts 13). But when he preached in Athens, he did not quote the Bible (see Acts 17). Instead, he quoted the Greek poets to illustrate what he was saying and he let their cultural context give a framework to his message.

We need to make sure that the meaning of our message is understood. As preachers let us do all we can to enter our listeners' world and speak their language so that they may understand the Good News and believe, and believing might have life in his name.

Be practical

Jesus asked blind Bartimaeus, 'What do you want me to do for you?' Many times Jesus discerned what people needed, as he did with the woman of Samaria or with Zacchaeus. Sometimes they asked him a question, like the rich ruler who was seeking eternal life. The man did not want eternal life enough to let his wealth go, so he went away disappointed and unchanged. Zacchaeus and the woman of Samaria saw that Jesus could meet their needs, and they believed in Jesus the Messiah, the Son of God.

Unless the new pearl is seen to be worth more than all the old ones, there will be a negative response. As we preach Jesus, we need to speak to what people are hungry for. We need to realize that people's most pressing need may not be for forgiveness first. They may need acceptance first, like Zacchaeus. They may need to be healed first, like the man at the pool of Bethesda. They may need physical safety first, like the Philippian jailer. Then they all came to need and want forgiveness, but that was not the need they first felt. We have to recognize the needs that people themselves feel and not act as though we know their needs better than they do.

In an ancient fable, the sun and the wind had a contest to see which of them could get a man to take off his coat. As the wind blew harder and harder, the man only drew his coat closer around him. Then the sun sent out its warmth and, in a short time, the man willingly took off his coat. Some preaching is like a cold wind to the hearers: it makes them more defensive. Preaching that is warm, that meets people's needs, adds motive to understanding and makes communication effective. We don't have to make the Bible relevant – it already is. But we do have to demonstrate its relevance by applying it to people's needs.

When all has been said and done, a lot more has been said than done. The purpose of preaching the gospel is that people might turn to Christ and be healed (Matt. 13:15). A key verse for every preacher is: 'Do not merely listen to the word, and so deceive yourselves. Do what it says' (James 1:22 NIV).

Several times Jesus concluded his preaching with the words, 'Now go and do likewise.' We need to make sure our preaching is not long on diagnosis and short on remedy. When I go to the doctor, I don't just want diagnosis, I want remedy. Christianity is more than a belief; it is behaviour. It is more than a creed; it is character and conduct. The active response that should follow preaching can be temporary or permanent: the seed that fell in good soil bore lasting fruit; the seed sown in the rocks and among thorns did not last. Jesus calls us to bear fruit that remains (John 15:16). Whether we get a life-transforming response from preaching, of course, depends on the work of the Holy Spirit. The Parable of the Sower, however, shows that the hearers' response is affected by how well they understand the message, and that hangs on us communicating effectively. It is not what people like about our talks and sermons that matters, but what they do after they have heard. If we as preachers desire for God's seed to fall on good soil and produce a harvest of transformed lives, we need to be aware of the needs and perceptions of our hearers. Telling the gospel story is not enough. We must communicate it in a way that reaches our listeners at their point of need and brings the Good News into focus for their lives.

Rather than being inspired to give the occasional evangelistic sermon, I would much prefer preachers always to preach and teach as if they were evangelists. Then thousands of churches would be fruitful.

Preaching evangelistically is not about clever ideas and clever techniques. I believe that if a preacher will take these four principles (be yourself, be prayerful, be clear and be practical), and apply them as they minister, and preach 'as if they were an evangelist', then the Lord will honour them, and they will see people turn to Christ.

In the words of the apostle Paul, who is an example to all of us as we seek to preach evangelistically, may God give you grace to preach the gospel not simply with words, but also with power, with the Holy Spirit and with deep conviction (1 Thess. 1:5)!

Chapter 2

A Picture is Worth a Thousand Words
The power of illustration in evangelism

J.John

> The best thing to do . . . is to speak in pictures, to recount stories and anecdotes. Rather than tell an audience that the Empire State Building is 1,454 feet high, create a picture: If you stacked 215 subway cars end to end they would be just a little bit taller than the Empire State Building. Many speakers only give you facts and figures. People cannot take all that in, but if you can include the same information within the context of a story or analogy, it is much easier for people to absorb. And it will capture their attention!
>
> Nicole Wells,
> Professor of Public Speaking, University of New York[1]

A vicar greeted his departing congregation by the church door. One old woman said to him, 'Your sermon this morning was like the peace and mercy of the Lord.' The vicar gave a self-satisfied smile which melted from his face as the woman continued, 'I thought it passed all understanding and would never come to an end!'

Many preachers fail to communicate effectively or hold the attention of their hearers simply because they speak in abstract theology with no illustrations. It is like all meat with no seasoning.

This chapter is about cultivating the art of using illustrations in your speaking. The best illustrations take the form of narrative – a simple story. It is my belief that many preachers could do with seasoning their sermons liberally in this way.

Jesus the great storyteller

Our example in this is Jesus himself – and much of this chapter will be applying lessons from his ministry of preaching.

Jesus appreciated a good story. The Bible records that Jesus never spoke without using a parable (Matt. 13:34). In other words, Jesus always communicated by telling a story. I want to be like Jesus. He consistently sprinkled his teaching with real-life situations and stories to effectively communicate his point, and people were 'amazed at his teaching' (Matt. 7:28 NIV). There was something compelling about the way Jesus communicated that created amazement.

Jesus built on what people already knew by using parables about familiar things. He understood people because he 'knew their thoughts'. We too need to know as much as we can about people. What kinds of things do we need to know? The range of Jesus' parables and sayings provides a good guide. They show that Jesus was good at observing people – careful at noticing what revolved around people's lives. And since the home, the family and work are the greater part of any person's life, Jesus knew a lot about bread-making; he knew that children liked fish and eggs, but not without salt; he knew how exciting weddings were and how heart-breaking funerals were; he knew about hostility and resentment between brothers. Jesus knew all about farming: ploughing, sowing, weeding, harvesting. Sheep, oxen and dogs all came into his examples. He knew about vines, figs and mustard trees. He was familiar with the market-place and with its merchants and traders. He was comfortable with working men – fishermen and soldiers. He observed social conditions: crime, the courts, the prisons, the banquets of the rich and the misery of the poor. He knew about sickness and doctors' bills. And nature made its impression on Jesus: the wind in the trees and lilies, sparrows, foxes, camels, wolves, serpents and their ways.

Be familiar but not predictable

A good story uses things that are *familiar* to the hearer – things drawn from life. Even the most illiterate, uneducated peasant could identify with the situations that Jesus described in his parables.

Jesus' use of the familiar didn't mean he was predictable. Jesus often told parables in a surprising way. With Jesus there was always the unexpected turn to the way he took the familiar and used it. It must have been great to be one of the crowd who heard Jesus preaching. Imagine them chatting among themselves as they are waiting for him to speak. 'I love Jesus' stories.' 'Yeah, I like the gardening ones.' 'No, I don't like the gardening ones, I like the political ones.' 'No, I like the ones where the parents tell their sons what to do but they don't do it.' 'Well, let's see what Jesus is going to tell us today.' Jesus tells a story (Luke 10:30ff):

Jesus: A certain man was going down from Jerusalem to Jericho . . .

Crowd: Well, that's not surprising. A lot of people travel on that road.

Jesus: . . . and he got attacked.

Crowd: Well, that's not surprising either: there are a lot of robbers hiding out in those bushes on that road.

Jesus: They attacked him and left him for dead.

Crowd: What?! This is going to be a sad story today! He hasn't told us a really sad story for a while.

Jesus: But a priest came that way . . .

Crowd: Oh, good! Our brother is going to live after all! The priest will look after him. That's part of his job, isn't it?

Jesus: . . . and he stopped . . .

Crowd: Yeah, of course. He would stop, wouldn't he?

Jesus: . . . and he looked. Then he walked by on the other side.

Crowd: Uh?! What kind of a story is this? What do you mean? Our brother is dying, the priest has stopped and looked. . . . But maybe the priest is busy. He's got lots of priestly things to do.

Jesus: But a Levite came along . . .

Crowd: Good, a Levite. A Levite doesn't have to do all those weddings and funerals. He's got more time. Our brother is going to receive the help he needs.

Jesus: . . . and the Levite stopped . . .

Crowd: Yeah, we knew he would stop.

Jesus: . . . and he looked, but then he walked by.

Crowd: Uh?! What kind of story is this? The priest comes, he looks, he walks away. The Levite comes, he looks, he walks away. . . . Ah, we know what kind of a story this is. It's the kind of story where the person you didn't think would help comes and helps. The underdog – yes, it's that kind of a story. The priest fails, the Levite fails, but an ordinary Jewish guy does the right thing.

Jesus: A Samaritan comes along . . .

Crowd: (*spitting on the floor*) If our brother isn't dead already, he will be now! And if the robbers have left anything behind, it will go now!

Jesus: . . . and the Samaritan stopped and he picked the man up. He put him on his donkey, he looked after him, poured oil on his wounds, fed him and gave him accommodation.

Crowd: We *never* heard of a story like *that* before!

The priest looks and walks away – *surprise*. The Levite looks and walks away – *surprise*. The Samaritan stops and shows compassion – *intense surprise*. Jesus throws in an unexpected twist. The contemporary equivalent would be: 'A member of Hamas was mugged on the West Bank and an Israeli came to his aid.'

In this retelling of the parable I am seeking to demonstrate the principle of trying to connect and engage with people in the same way that Jesus did. When Jesus told stories there was always interaction.

Preach in a way that raises questions

Jesus' parables were stories, and everyone likes a good story. Good story-telling heightens interest. And what is very interesting with Jesus is that he left a lot to his hearers' imagination. When Jesus' disciples asked him why he used parables, he explained that the stories enabled those people with an open heart to hear what God wanted them to hear, while those people with hardened hearts were kept in the dark (Matt. 13:10ff).

Jesus' teaching style was *inductive*. Have you ever noticed just how many questions he asked? He did this not because he needed to know the answer but because they did. He did this to draw them out.

His teaching fascinated and intrigued his disciples, leading them to have their hearts and minds illuminated, by allowing *them* to reflect on the meaning of his parables for themselves.

In this way the people ended up saying things to themselves that they would have resented if he had said them directly. Jesus didn't have the urge that most preachers have to say it *all* every time. Listeners are like a radio: they have an off switch. They can totally switch the preacher off. It was this type of person that Jesus was referring to when he spoke of the seed falling on the hard-trodden path. The truth did not even get a hearing. It was screened out. Knowledge of our audience and the skill to build on what they already know in a way that captures their curiosity are essential factors in getting their attention.

Be graphic as well as verbal

Jesus' teaching was often graphic as well as verbal. He used object lessons such as bread and wine to symbolize his death, or drawing in the sand, or putting spit in a blind man's eyes. In this way he turned some of his teaching into *enacted parables*.

I used the following illustration in a men's prison. Holding up a new £50 note (I have also used this analogy with a $100 bill in the US), I said:

> I've got a brand new £50 note. Who would like this £50? Please put your hand up if you would like it. I would like to give this to somebody. The note is clean and crisp. So what I am going to do is crease it up. [*I make a show of creasing up the note.*]
>
> Now, who wants a creased £50 note? Hands up! It was worth £50 when it was nice and clean, but now that it is all creased up, it's still worth £50. It hasn't lost its value.
>
> But it's still clean – it needs some dirt. [*I make a show of making the note dirty.*] Who wants a dirty, creased £50 note?
>
> So, you do still want it? It was worth £50 when it was clean and crisp and then, when I creased it, it didn't lose its value. It was still worth £50. Then I dirtied it, but it still didn't lose its value. It's still worth £50.
>
> It doesn't matter how creased you and I feel, it doesn't matter how dirty you and I feel our lives are – you and I have never lost our value in God's eyes.

When I got to the punchline the men in the prison started shouting, 'I'm valuable!' and kept on shouting it! The illustration then enabled me to communicate how the Lord cleanses our lives.

Isn't that the message of Christianity? We may feel we have lost our value, but the gospel shows us that in God's eyes we are still as valuable as ever.

And on that occasion I went on and explained that we are all guilty of being dirty (sin), and the big question is, what do we do about it?

> Some people try to deflect it – blame other people. Some people deny it and say they are not personally responsible. Some people drown it in drink and drugs.

Then a pause. . . . There can be an awesome, sacred silence during a pause.

> We can only deal with guilt by dissolving it in the blood of Jesus.

I find that the situations in which I am communicating to all ages – for example, family services – are the most difficult. The following simple Christmas message is an example of an approach that can be used in an all-age setting. Having made a giant Christmas cracker, which is quite easy to do, I say:

> I have got a cracker here and I need a couple of people to help me pull it. Who wants to come and help me? [*Pull the cracker with the volunteers.*]
>
> When we pull a cracker, what comes out? Three things: a hat, a message and a present. [*Put the hat on.*]
>
> Later today, at Christmas dinner when you put your hat on, I want you to remember it isn't a hat, it's a crown. The reason it's a crown is because a King has been born.
>
> The second thing you get in a cracker is a message. Normally you get a stupid little message, but today I want you to remember that the message of Christmas is: A Saviour has been born to us today.
>
> And when you receive your little gift, I want you to remember that the gift of Christmas is Christ.
>
> So I want you to remember those three things. See if you can remember them at Christmas lunch today.

No matter whether the person hearing this message is a senior citizen, a middle-aged adult, a teenager or a four-year-old, they will take something home with them about the message of Christmas.

It is my perception that as preachers we are often very good at the presentation of the message, but we are not very good at pulling in the net and helping people to take the step of becoming a Christian. Recently, on an occasion when I was speaking evangelistically, I used this illustration before making an appeal:

> A man and a woman were making their vows during their marriage ceremony. The vicar asked the groom, 'Will you take this woman to be your lawful wedded wife?'
>
> He replied, 'Well, I've been thinking, actually. . . .'
>
> The vicar responded, 'Well, it's good that you have been thinking, but actually I have asked you a question: "Will you?"'
>
> The groom said, 'Well, I get very excited when I think about her.'
>
> And the vicar persisted, 'I'm very glad you get excited when you think about her, but the question I am asking you is, "Will you?"'
>
> And the man said, 'I will.'
>
> The vicar then turned to the bride and asked, 'Will you take this idiot to be your lawful wedded husband?'

This little anecdote was like the cherry on top of a cake. I followed on by saying, 'Look, you may be thinking about what you have heard and your heart may have been stirred, but it is a question of the will. Will you?'

Somebody came up to me afterwards and said, 'J.John, I've got to speak to you.' He told me that he had become a Christian and that it was that final illustration that was the 'tipping-point' that enabled him to make a commitment to Christ. The cherry helped that man to receive the cake!

I believe we need to become better equipped in knowing how to explain the gospel in such a way that we will see people come through to faith.

Following a sermon one Easter Day, a woman came up to me and told me with great excitement, 'I had an epiphany – I hadn't seen it before.' The aspect of my sermon that had sparked off the revelation of which she was speaking was simply this:

> People will often ask, 'Why Jesus?'
>
> You are walking down a street which branches into two and you don't know which way to go – left or right. You are really confused, you just don't know which way to go.
>
> There are two men lying there – one's dead, one's alive. Which one would you ask for directions?

It was this simple explanation that enabled the woman to see the truth for the first time. The Holy Spirit takes our illustrations and illuminates people's minds and hearts.

Open an illustrations bank account

Sometimes people say to me, 'Where do you find all these stories?' I think I find them because I am constantly on the look-out for them. We all need to learn to look out for resources and then to bank them.

I am bit like a squirrel when it comes to stories. I am continually collecting and saving. As preachers, we are not going to be able to draw from the bank if there are no resources in our account. It is a mind-set, an attitude, which all preachers and speakers need to develop. As preachers who are endeavouring to season our sermons, I believe that we need to access the resources that are becoming increasingly available. They can provide us with good stories and illustrations to enable us to make our point, or they can be used to change the atmosphere or set the scene for what we want to say. We can take the story or illustration and make it our own by putting ourselves into it.

Effective communication is not difficult if we follow the principles outlined in this chapter and cultivate the art of illustrating truth with narrative. I believe that, if God can speak through a donkey, he can speak through anything! He has chosen to speak through *us*, so let's follow the example of Jesus the story-teller so that we might be a more effective mouthpiece for him. We should pray:

> Thank you, Lord, that you have showed us how to cook the meat. Please help us to put some seasoning on it.
>
> Lord, thank you for giving us the recipe to create the cake. Please help us now to put on the icing with the cherry on top!
>
> Amen.

Chapter 3

This is My Story
The use of testimony in evangelism

Barry Woodward

> It is truly hard to believe that this was written by a politician. It is such a good read and provides such a thoughtful and open account of Obama's views and experiences, that it is truly breathtaking.
>
> Review of *Dreams from my Father*, the autobiography of Barack Obama[1]

You only have to walk into a bookstore to see that people are fascinated by other people's life stories. Often the biography/autobiography section is vast. As with Barack Obama's best-selling book, autobiographies are a testimony to what a person believes, what makes them tick and how they came to be the person they are.

One newspaper motto is: 'People want to read about people.' This is nothing new. Two thousand years ago, Jesus knew that people liked to hear about other people's stories. That's why, when he was preaching, he told stories, usually about people. In this chapter I will explore the why and how of testimony – why testimony is important and how to go about delivering one.

The why of testimony

1. Testimony demonstrates relevance

Stories of human interest are an essential way of communicating Christianity in today's society.

Traditionally, we have called a person's *faith story* their *testimony*. Some have suggested that using faith stories in evangelism is outmoded, but I firmly believe nothing could be further from the truth.

As a travelling evangelist, I do a lot of short-term missions and one-off speaking engagements in local churches. At times, depending on the event, I will invite friends and colleagues to contribute to meetings by sharing their stories.

Some time ago I heard that there was one particular man who had quite an interesting story, so I asked him if he would like to join me on one of my missions. He told me he would get back to me. Two weeks later I phoned him to ask if he had decided whether he wanted to come and tell his story. His reply was, 'I've been thinking about it and I don't really do my testimony any more; I've grown out of that.'

Strange that he felt he had outgrown one of the main ways in which secular people communicate today. If we find the term *testimony* old-fashioned, let's think of a faith story as a *spiritual autobiography*. This is clearly not outmoded, as the review of President Obama's autobiography makes clear.

2. Testimony makes truth more accessible

Few people are interested in abstract truth, but a story can concretize the same truths in a much more palatable way.

Our own personal stories (our micro-narratives) can play a key role in our evangelistic strategy of reaching the unreached with God's story (the meta-narrative) – the Good News of Jesus Christ.

The apostle Paul also realized this in his day. While Peter was a fisherman, Paul was an intellectual and was responsible for writing the largest portion of the New Testament – teaching aimed at *Christians* that, at times, is direct propositional truth (logical theological statements).

Theologians call this 'non-public *kerygma*' (*kerygma* means 'proclamation'). This was his in-house teaching for those already in the faith.

Yet propositional truth is not the only means that Paul uses to communicate. The Book of Acts records Paul telling his life story *three* times – no doubt he told it many more times during his ministry. On each of these occasions he was speaking to a *non-Christian* audience. This is called 'public *kerygma*' – Paul's preaching to those (as yet) outside the faith.

The way Paul communicated to a *private Christian* audience was different to the way he communicated to a *public non-Christian* audience. When speaking to the not-yet-Christian group, more often than not he used his own personal story to help people connect to God's story.

3. *Testimony has power*

Revelation 12:11 states: 'They overcame him [the devil] by the blood of the Lamb and by the word of their testimony' (NIV).

In a court of law a witness who is called to the stand is there to give a *testimony* – an honest account of what they have seen and heard.

This is what we as Christians are called to do – to give our personal account of our little bit in God's big story and to testify to what he has done in our lives. A testimony in a court of law has power of a legal kind. A spiritual testimony has power of a spiritual kind – as the verse in Revelation states – to even overcome the work of the evil one.

In Luke 8:39 Jesus healed the demon-possessed man and then he said to him, 'Return home and tell how much God has done for you' (NIV). And so the man went off and told everyone how much Jesus had done for him. He became a living witness to what God had done in his life.

4. Testimony is for everyone

I travel around the UK meeting lots of different people, all of whom have their own story to tell. I don't think I have ever met two people who have the same story. That's because each of us is unique and God works in us all in different ways. My story is my story and your story is your story; no two stories are the same. We all have a story to tell.

I often say this: 'There are two types of people in the church: those who can stand up and testify to what God has "saved" them from and those who can stand up and testify to what God has "kept" them from.'

I would fall into the *saved from* group. I left school with no qualifications, became a drug addict and dealer, spent time in various prisons, had a string of broken relationships and then, after fourteen years of addiction, I had a life-changing encounter with God. Even though there are quite a few stories like mine around, we are still the minority of people in the church.

On the other hand, my wife Tina didn't take drugs, she has never been in prison, she worked hard at school and then later got herself a degree at university. The way she lived her life was the complete opposite of the way I lived my life (a wise woman – you can see why I married her!). She would fall into the *kept from* group; these are the majority of people in the church. Our stories are completely opposite but we both have a story to tell.

When people from the *kept from* group have heard my story, they have sometimes bewailed the fact that they 'do not have a testimony'. Listen – if you belong to Christ, you have a valid testimony, no matter *what* your story is – whether you have been brought up a Christian, have gone to church all your life, had a gradual conversion – whatever. You have a story and it's worth telling!

The only valid testimony is an authentic one, and a story of a gradual spiritual dawning to an upper-class lady whose only vice was reading Mills & Boon novels will connect with people when I cannot!

The how of testimony

Having looked at these four principles of why testimony is important, I now want to share six tips for how to go about giving your testimony in a public setting.

Often people assume that because it's their own spiritual autobiography and they know it, all they have to do is stand up and speak it out. Well, for the majority of people who are not used to public speaking, this is not the case if it is to be done well.

Even if you are never called upon to do this, it is still a useful exercise to prepare your story as I suggest, because it allows you to get it clear in your own mind for when you share it informally.

What are the keys to maximizing effectiveness?

1. Have a basic structure

Like any other kind of public address, our personal stories need a structure: to put it simply – a beginning, a middle and an end. The structure that I have found useful for my story is:

1. BC – Before Conversion (before you gave your life to Christ).
2. DC – During Conversion (how you came to give your life to Christ).
3. AC – After Conversion (since you've given your life to Christ).

When we use a structure for our story, it will help

- the listener to follow the narrative from beginning to end;
- to stop the story-teller from jumping back and forth to different times and events in their life;
- to give a balanced picture of your whole life story;
- cut out unnecessary waffle;
- the speaker know when to end;
- to stop you preaching rather than testifying (if you're not the main speaker).

2. Be creative

Even though I stick to the simple structure I have outlined, when telling my story *there is an exception*. Have you ever read an autobiography that starts with birth, infancy and childhood, and you wished it would hurry up and get to the interesting bits?

In 2007 my autobiography, *Once an Addict*, was published and we started to organize book-launch events that were strategically evangelistic. In the first chapter of the book, I tell the story of the time when I got busted for possession of heroin, while I was on remand in Strangeways Prison. After I tell this story, I go right back to my childhood and unfold my story from the beginning.

I find that people are often gripped by the first story I tell, and they are then with me all the way through because they want to know how I got put in prison in the first place, and then ultimately how I became a Christian.

3. Tailor your story to fit the occasion

When it comes to giving a testimony, one size definitely does not fit all!

You may have been in a meeting when a person giving a testimony went on far too long. Not only did this irritate the organizers (and the main speaker if it reduced his or her time), but also it ended up robbing the testimony of its effectiveness, as it was not fit for purpose. The way round this is to think about timings that are appropriate to a given occasion.

My approach to this is to have three different adaptations of my faith story at hand:

1. The News Flash version. This lasts between 3 and 5 minutes and gives just the headlines of my life. *This is suitable for a testimony slot.*
2. The *News at Ten* adaptation. This lasts between 30 and 40 minutes and gives the headlines, some commentary, and the gospel message with an opportunity for people to respond (this is the one I'm most often asked for). *This is suitable for a sermon slot.*

3. The Documentary adaptation. This can last anything up to an hour or more. This gives the headlines, commentary, some of the finer details of my story, and the gospel with response. *This is suitable for a special event*.

As you can see, the setting will determine which adaptation I use. There was one occasion when I was involved with a programme on God TV called the *Frost Debate* – a programme produced by the late Rob Frost. The filming took place at Easter People (a large Christian conference) in Blackpool. After Rob Frost had interviewed me, he asked what I was doing for the rest of the day, because he wanted me to tell my story in one of the evening meetings. After making a few changes to my schedule, I stayed on so that I could speak that evening. I wasn't the main speaker and I was given a five-minute slot to testify, so I did the News Flash version of my story – I just told them the headlines. If I had been the main speaker and had been specifically asked to tell my whole story, I would have used either the *News at Ten* adaptation or the Documentary one, depending on the time allocated to me. The setting will always determine which one I use.

4. Make it present, not just past

I have heard many people get up to tell their stories, and they spend 30 minutes telling you all about what they were like before they became a Christian, and then they stop at the point when they became one!

This isn't an effective witness, as for many people the big issue is not 'Is this Jesus stuff true?' but 'Does this Jesus stuff work?' What difference does being a Christian make to daily life?

It's important to spend a balanced amount of time on each section of your story (see point 1 above). So, if I were telling the 5-minute News Flash version of my story, I would use 2 minutes talking about what I was like *before conversion*, 2 minutes talking about *during conversion* and then 1 minute sharing about what my life has been like *after conversion*. If I was using my 40-minute *News at Ten* adaptation, I would allot 10 minutes each to the first 3 sections and then 10 minutes to the gospel message and response.

5. Work on presentation, not just the content

If we are going to be effective at telling our personal story, we need to present it well – not just paying attention to *what* we say but also to *how* we say it. How we deliver it will have an effect on the outcome.

One day, I was sitting on the front row at a church, waiting to get up to speak, when the pastor got up and invited one of his church members to tell his story. The man left his chair and made his way to the platform.

After taking the microphone, looking at the end, tapping it and then asking, 'Is this on?', he looked out to the crowd and said, 'Are you alright? Praise the Lord! Halleluiah! Jesus is alive!'

He then proceeded to tell everyone how great Jesus was and how good it was to be 'saved from his sin', while holding the mike about waist height, which rendered it an electronic cosmetic accessory. After a long introduction, full of Christian jargon, he said that he used to be a 'drunk', but Jesus had set him free.

During this time he seemed fixated on one particular section of the room (making the people there feel he was preaching to them), not making eye contact with anybody else. Then he started to tell people that they needed Jesus. 'We all need Jesus,' he kept repeating, over and over again.

I was sitting there sinking further and further back into my seat with each sentence that he spoke. I was embarrassed not only for him but also for the many unchurched visitors who were in the meeting.

Here are a few things to remember when presenting your story:

- Start well (know your opening sentence before you stand up to speak).
- Smile (if you look as if you are enjoying yourself, others will too)!
- Speak *English*, not *Christianese* – no religious jargon (remember, you are speaking to the non-Christians in the audience, not the Christians).
- Make eye contact with the crowd and scan the audience (don't just look at one section of the audience).
- Don't preach (that's the main speaker's job).
- Avoid nervous mannerisms (don't play with your notes, the microphone, your hair, or your watch, or make excessive hand gestures).
- Hold the microphone properly (about five inches under your mouth).
- Relax (don't be stiff, move around a little)!
- Avoid verbal speech filters ('errrm', 'er', 'OK', 'right' or tutting).
- Use wit (self-deprecating humour is always a winner).
- Finish well (plan how you are going to come in to land).

6. Rely on his power

All this tuition on how to give your faith story can make the prospect a little daunting. We need to be mindful at all times of Jesus' promise as we seek to step out and be obedient to his call to be his witnesses. Acts 1:8 records the risen Christ's famous last words to his disciples:

> But you will receive power when the Holy Spirit comes on you; and you will be my witnesses in Jerusalem, and in all Judea and Samaria, and to the ends of the earth (NIV).

It is sometimes said that where there's a promise there's a premise. His promise of power is in the very context of being his witnesses, so we can be confident that as *we go* Christ goes *with us*. Do we sometimes wonder why, when we are filled with the Spirit afresh at church, the experience soon wanes and we feel spiritually dry again? Acts 1:8 would suggest that we need to do something with it!

Let's step out in faith and in the power of his Spirit and use our unique faith-story for him – whether from the pulpit or in informal conversation – that it might demonstrate that Jesus is alive and still in the business of changing lives even today!

Chapter 4

Divine Comedy
Using humour in evangelism

Mark Greenwood

> It's my belief that humour is one of the greatest agents we have for good in this world. Humour is vital to human life, and probably always has been. It is timeless, and occurs in all cultures.
>
> Gerry Maguire Thompson[1]

Aristotle studied it, Socrates debated it and Darwin wrote a paper on his theory of it! Freud and, more recently, Woody Allen have tried to formulate a clear explanation of the purpose of it. There has been more research into it in the last twenty-five years than in all previous centuries combined. Today, we are more diverse in our opinion of it and how it works than we have ever been. It's one of the greatest forms of communication and entertainment. It's attempted by many and mastered by few, and yet the ability to make people laugh is one of the most sought-after things in the world.

As a youngster I watched stand-up comedians and impressionists, and envied their ability to make people laugh. I remember trying to emulate them. I would regularly disappear into the cellar in our terraced house in

Bradford and return only moments later, donning a flat cap turned back to front and uttering the immortal words, 'Mmm, Betty!' (the motto of the legendary Frank Spencer, for the uninitiated). I've always enjoyed making people laugh and it stood me in good stead through my secondary school. At the age of 17, I left Bradford to train as an evangelist, and it was then that I began to use humour in evangelism and immediately saw its potential. Twenty years later, I am more convinced than I have ever been that humour can be highly effective in communicating the gospel.

In this chapter I want to share with you some of my discoveries and experiences as I have both practised and studied humour in my ministry as an evangelist. I can only whet your appetite in the space I have available, and so I would encourage you to be 'serious about humour' and learn the craft yourself through study and practice.

God invented humour!

A friend of mine was on a placement at a church while he was training to be a vicar. He had preached a sermon that was faithful to the Bible and had everyone laughing as well. At the end, an old woman came to give the young trainee minister some advice: 'Your job is to communicate what the Spirit is saying to the churches – and he's not telling jokes!'

It sounds spiritual, doesn't it? But is humour really incompatible with preaching?

Someone asked a newspaper, 'Are there any jokes in the Bible?' Well, the answer is simple – yes! The Bible has more humour in it than we might think. Many of the Proverbs told great truths with humour. Jesus told many parables; this was a key way of communicating. They weren't told in an uninteresting way – in fact, quite the opposite. They were more in the genre of a witty storyteller and would most definitely have involved banter. Some of the sayings of Christ had humorous observations – what we would now call observational humour. His comments would have had people laughing while making a serious point. Take the story of the shepherd leaving the ninety-nine to find the one. Shepherds were the butt of Galilean society's jokes, so this story would have raised a laugh. Putting it into a modern-day setting: 'Did you hear the one about the shepherd who left ninety-nine sheep to find just one?'

Jesus' use of hyperbole is comic genius. In Matthew 23:24 he says, 'You strain out a gnat but swallow a camel' (NIV). In Matthew 7:3 he says, 'Why do you look at the speck of sawdust in your brother's eye and pay no attention to the plank in your own eye?' (NIV). This is great material for any cartoonist. The Gospels are full of these humorous pictures that Jesus, the greatest and most influential person who ever lived, saw fit to use.

Humour is not the only way to communicate, but it is a brilliant way, and will certainly add seasoning to any talk. It is biblical and doesn't make light of the gospel, as some people might think. Nor is it a modern phenomenon, as some suggest – as if the giants of the past would definitely not be amused! The 'prince of preachers', C. H. Spurgeon, who is often quoted because of his brilliant expository preaching, also used humour. In fact, a whole chapter in his autobiography is devoted to humour in preaching.

Some of the most prominent contemporary communicators of the Christian faith, such as J.John, Nicky Gumbel, Eric Delve, Jeff Lucas, Mike Pilavachi and many others, use humour to great effect.

In my case, three strangers in three places have encouraged me to continue with humour.

I try to hone my humour by occasionally doing stand-up in secular clubs. I had done my routine at a comedy club in Stafford, and at the end of the evening a woman came up to me and told me that she hadn't intended coming this evening, as she had had the worst week of her life, but she decided to come anyway. The first performer (a professional comedian) had gone on stage and, in her words, 'He didn't even make me smile, but when you got up I saw something different in you, and something inside me broke.'

In Cardiff, I had finished my talk at the beginning of a mission week. An older woman came up to me at the end and uttered the words, 'You will never know what you have done for me this morning.' One of the leaders told me the significance of her words. The woman had had an operation some years previously which had not gone well. This had caused deep sorrow and meant that she had not laughed for around five years. That morning she laughed like she had never laughed before.

In Birmingham, I had just spoken to a hundred women at an evangelistic event. I was speaking to those who had responded when a woman came to see me. She said, 'You made me laugh so much tonight, you have inspired me to believe in God.'

Why use humour?

The humorist Victor Borge said, 'Laughter is the shortest distance between two people.'

1. To make a connection

One of the first things I learnt in my evangelism training (evangelism has been the all-consuming focus in my preaching and the reason for my work in stand-up comedy) is based on Deuteronomy 31:12: 'Assemble the people – men, women and children, and the aliens living in your towns – so that they can listen and learn to fear the LORD your God and follow carefully all the words of this law' (NIV).

This verse is an encouragement to assemble the people so they can listen. It's not enough just to gather people physically; we must also engage them mentally. Once we have done that, we need to keep their attention so they can listen. In other words – get their attention and keep their interest. I find this is best done with humour. When you make people laugh or smile, you've made a connection. When you make a connection, it is amazing what you can download. You can smuggle in the gospel. Conversely, when you lose the connection, you can't communicate.

2. To establish common ground

Jesus told many parables, which were earthly stories with a heavenly meaning. Our humorous stories are modern parables. Using this technique is an attempt to find a place of common ground and agreement so that we can then take the hearer to a place that is uncommon ground and a possible place of disagreement. I would rather start where people are at and take them to where I want them to be. Humour does this exceptionally well.

3. To put people at ease

An unbeliever said to me at the end of a talk, 'You have an amazing ability to put people at ease.' Many people who are unbelievers, listening to a talk about God, feel that they are in an alien environment. Especially in a church service, where so much of what is said and done is not part of their culture, humour is a brilliant way of putting people at ease.

I have absolutely no problem with people feeling awkward because the Holy Spirit is working on them, but I don't want it to be because they feel like a pork pie at a bar mitzvah! It is less likely that they will feel this way if we can make them laugh or at least put a smile on their face.

4. To be winsome

Humour is winsome and often makes people like you! If they like you it is more likely that they will listen to what you are talking about and agree with you. I do believe that the more you make people laugh, the harder you can 'hit them' with the gospel. Once again, I have no problem with people not liking the gospel, but I don't want it to be because they don't like me!

5. To demolish misconceptions

The first point on the Alpha supper talk is: 'Christianity: *Boring* . . .' I'm so glad Nicky Gumbel starts here, because for many people Christianity *is* boring. They don't get to discover whether it is irrelevant or untrue because their first impression is that there is more fun to be had watching paint dry!

If somebody isn't yet ready to become a Christian, but their preconceived negative misconceptions are blown out of the water, then we should see that as a result! I could not begin to count the number of people who have told me that their non-Christian friends came to the event, and though they didn't come to faith, they said it was the best night out they'd ever had. These are thrilling words to hear from somebody when you have just told them that they are separated from God by the wrong that they do and that they need Jesus.

Genres of humour

There is much subjective talk as to what actually makes something funny. In reality, it is one of the great unknowns. It is possible to tell *unfunny* jokes and make people laugh, just as it is possible to tell *funny* jokes even though you aren't funny. The disaster is when you are not funny and you tell an unfunny joke. Just think of the speeches at many a wedding reception (or maybe you'd rather not)! Gag-telling is a craft and more difficult to master. The development of the observational humour of today's alternative comedians (such as Billy Connolly) has made it a bit easier, because if you tell a story and it doesn't work, you have the narrative to fall back on.

Here are some genres of humour and some examples of them.

1. The unexpected

Two of the best comedy sketches are the greatest examples of this. Del Boy is in a bar with his friend, Trig. Del Boy is trying to impress some ladies. He's standing by the bar and tells Trig to 'act cool'. At that moment one of the bar staff lifts up the bar flap to come out from behind the bar. Del Boy leans to prop up the bar and, without flinching, falls through the gap – a brilliant comedy moment!

I sometimes use this technique to introduce myself. I say, 'When I was younger I thought about what I would do when I got older. I thought to myself, "I'd love to be a policeman" – but I wasn't tall enough.' I am five feet six – people smile and gently chuckle. I go on to say, 'I thought I'd become a footballer, but I resembled the football more than the footballer.' I am portly in stature, so they chuckle a bit more. Then I say, 'So I thought to myself, "I know, I'll get a job working with animals" – so I became a butcher.' Now they laugh – I did actually become a butcher.

2. The familiar

Next time you're with an old friend, mention people you knew or something that you did when you were young or something that was a fad or trend then and is no longer around. Then watch as, at the very least, you bring a smile to their face and they probably laugh. The use of the familiar is a great way to make people laugh. One of the great exponents of this is Peter Kay. Much of his brilliant material is based on this and has people all around the country reciting his routines.

3. Observation

There is lots of humour in everyday life. Observation is similar to familiarity but more difficult, as there is a risk that people won't see it as you do. Peter Kay does touch on this but Jack Dee is absolutely superb at it. Sit down with a pen and choose a subject like shopping and write down all your observations. Write about the relationship of people and what they say to each other and see what you come up with. The husband-and-wife dynamic is a sure-fire winner.

4. The extreme of the normal

Lee Evans has many routines to this effect. He will state something perfectly normal like, 'Why do we do this when we ask for the bill in a restaurant?' (as he says 'this' he mimics what many of us do, which is to write with an imaginary pen in the air). People are now laughing at something we all do which is normal. Then he says, 'Why do we do that? We don't do that when we are ordering the meal. We don't say, "I'll have the chicken"' – at this he walks around like a chicken, saying, 'I'll have the chicken, I'll have the chicken.'

What he has done is to take the normal into another situation, which shows its absurdity. This is the bread and butter of satire. It is essential for humour to contain both realism and exaggeration. It's good to start from a true point so the audience can associate with it. Then they are willing to suspend their disbelief.

5. Confused meaning

The Two Ronnies excelled at this in sketches like 'Four Candles' and 'Mastermind', where Ronnie Corbet answers the current question with the answer from the previous question. This is the staple of the very British genre of farce.

An example of this which I sometimes use is a well-known story called 'The WC'. Here it is so you can see it at work:

> A well-to-do English lady was planning a trip to Germany. She was registered to stay in a small, quiet house owned by the local schoolmaster and his wife. She was concerned as to whether or not the guest house contained a WC (water closet). She wrote the schoolmaster a letter, inquiring into the location of the WC.
>
> The schoolmaster, not a fluent speaker of English, asked the local parish priest if he knew the meaning of 'WC'. Together they pondered possible meanings of the

letters and finally concluded that the lady must be inquiring as to whether there was a wayside chapel near the house. The schoolmaster wrote the following letter in reply:

Dear Madam

I take great pleasure in informing you that the WC is situated 10 miles away from the house in the centre of a beautiful grove of pine trees, surrounded by lovely grounds. It is capable of holding 229 people and it is open on Sundays and Thursdays.

As there are a great number of people expected during the summer months, I suggest that you come early, although usually there is plenty of standing-room. This is an unfortunate situation, especially if you are in the habit of going regularly.

It may be of some interest to you to know that my daughter was married in that very WC and also that she met her husband there. I can remember the rush for seats. Why, there were ten people to every seat usually occupied by one. It was wonderful to see the expressions on their faces.

You will be glad to hear that a good number of people bring their lunch and make a day of it, while others wait until the last minute and arrive just on time. I would especially recommend your ladyship to go on Thursdays when there is organ accompaniment. The acoustics are excellent, and even the most delicate sounds can be heard everywhere. The newest addition is a bell, which rings every time a person enters. A bazaar is soon to be held to raise money to provide plush seats for all, since the people feel it is long needed.

My wife has been ill, and so she hasn't been able to go recently. It has been almost a year since she went last, which naturally pains her very much.

I shall be delighted to reserve the best seat for you, where you shall be seen by all. In fact, I look forward to escorting you there myself.

With kindest regards
The Schoolmaster

6. Real-life mishaps

These are fantastically hilarious and so a sure-fire winner. They are simply funny in and of themselves. Books such as *The Darwin Awards, The Book of Criminal Blunders* and *The Book of Heroic Failures* all sell well on this basis. I would suggest this as one of the best ways to use comedy in your talk, as these stories take little or no work and you're not telling a joke, so if you don't get a huge laugh, it's not a problem.

Here is an example of one such story that I use. I would tell it thus:

> I read a story of how, as part of a scuba-diving course, a trainee had to locate the instructor on the murky ocean floor and 'rescue' him. The instructor assured her that, like a panicking person, he would simulate struggle. After allowing her trainer a minute's start, the trainee found him, removed his air regulator, clasped him firmly and ascended slowly to the surface, while giving him air from her regulator every second breath. True to his word, he kicked and fought strenuously – and revealed, on pulling off his mask, that he was a complete stranger.

7. Personal mishaps

Your own personal mishaps are much funnier. These work even better because we are all basically very nosey and love finding out about people's lives. And quite apart from anything else, isn't it strangely encouraging to observe that other people are as foolish and daft as you? An added plus is that this is self-deprecating humour, which is very British (so it culturally connects), as well as not being negative about someone else. These stories can really engage the listener, because they are from your life and so the emotion comes through. Here is one of my personal mishaps:

> When I was about 18 years old, I went to see a friend, whose house I had only been to once before. He was a particularly good friend and we always called each other names. He urged me just to walk straight into his house and not bother knocking.
>
> Upon arriving at his house, I walked through the front door and shouted, 'Oi, Fatty! [I don't know why I called him this, as he was stick thin.] Put the kettle on!'
>
> Nothing happened, so I shouted again, 'Oi, Fatty! Put the kettle on!'
>
> Nothing happened, so I shouted really loudly, 'Oi, Fatty! Put the kettle on!'
>
> A woman appeared at the door of the living-room. She was not my friend's mum. This was largely due to the fact that this was not his house! I had gone into the wrong house, and his house was next door. (The two houses had front doors of the same colour.)
>
> I never did get my cup of tea!

How to use humour effectively

There you are, minding your own business, and somebody comes and tells you a joke. They trip over the words, or forget the main bit, or forget it completely and tell it wrong, or the joke is just not funny. The proverbial tumbleweed blows across the eternal silence, which is finally broken by your wise words, 'Ah well, it's the way you tell 'em!'

Here are a few pointers to help you avoid such scenarios, which would be counter-productive in communication:

1. Launch and land your stories

Whatever type of humour you use, make sure that you set it up properly. A simple way of doing this is by asking a question that is linked to the story you're telling. Let me give you an example of this by using a true story:

> A fisherman in the Aral Sea was out in his boat one day, when he was disturbed by a flying cow. Out of the blue, a Frisian landed on his boat, destroying it and almost drowning him. Of course, nobody believed him. The insurance company refused to pay out, and it was even reported in the newspaper that he told tall stories. Until, that is, the US Air Force admitted that a cow in one of their transport planes had gone mad and had been jettisoned over the Aral Sea.

When I use this story I start by saying, quite of the blue, 'Does anyone believe in flying cows? Put your hand up. I do – I believe in flying cows.' I then tell the story and finish with this landing: 'Believe the unbelievable, however unbelievable it may seem.'

2. Tell your jokes as stories

Don't say, 'Let me tell you a joke.' If you do, you've already set yourself up for a potential fall!

Though your hearers aren't saying it aloud, there is a mental response of, 'Come on then, make me laugh.' In reality, jokes are stories, so tell them as such. Try using phrases like, 'Somebody told me this story', 'I read this the other day', 'I heard of how . . .', to start the story. This technique takes people along a journey of a true situation that they can imagine themselves in. Then, when the punchline comes in (remember it!), it comes more as an unexpected turn. That is a component of humour.

3. Change your pace

Your humour can be used to change the pace of your talk. Sometimes I read the story even though I know it. This may be because I have been quite serious for some time and feel that a breather is necessary. I tend to use the humour at the beginning of a new point. In this way I have landed my last point and now I want to start off again in neutral, then to first, second, third, fourth and fifth gear, where I am preaching hard again.

A non-Christian said to me once, 'When I analyse what you said, you really hit me hard, but somehow I didn't realize because of how you did it.' I certainly find that the more you make them laugh, the more directly you can preach the gospel.

4. Expect a variety of responses

Sometimes you use a humorous story with one audience and it goes down really well. Another time, it doesn't seem to have gone down quite as well. Sometimes there is just no reason for this.

I remember talking with a secular professional comedian at a gig I was doing. This man was out four or five nights a week doing pretty well the same routine each night, so it was obviously very polished. When I was chatting to him at the end I asked him if he ever had any bad nights. He told me that about one in fifty were tougher nights. I asked him how he handled it and whether it was disheartening. He simply said, 'It's just a bad day at the office. I dig deep and get through it.'

Do everything you can to make your humour work, but remember that the reaction will vary.

5. Practise before the pulpit

Try your humour out on your friends first. There is a risk with this – you may end up annoying your friends! Humour is an important part of who I am. It's my default setting, even when I'm with friends – and it has to be controlled at times. Sometimes when I am out with them I may tell a story I've read or a bit of routine I'm working on or wanting to use. This can give me a good idea of how good it is, or isn't!

6. Be intentional about structure

As communicators of the gospel, we aren't using the humour just to make people laugh. It is crucial, therefore, that the humour we use takes our hearers on a journey to the point that we want to make.

There are two ways to use humour when preaching. In certain events it may be appropriate to make humour the backbone of your talk. In other words, your talk is like a comedy routine. The other way is that you have a formal sermon but your humour is illustrative of the points that you are making. Whichever way you use, have it clear in your mind and stick to it.

I have three places I want to take people: first, to a place where they recognize their problem – that is, their sin; second, to a place where they see that there is a remedy for their problem – that is, the cross; and third, to a place where they see that they need to respond to their predicament – that is, the decision to turn away from sin and to Christ.

Whether it's a stand-up-based talk or a formal talk with lots of humour, we need to make sure that it is structured for the gospel. I have a very clear and thought-through structure for my humour. I am very intentional about my choice of words and humorous illustrations, and I structure my humour in this way:

- *Head*: a point that reaches the mind (make this as humorous and creative as possible).
- *Heart*: humorous routines/stories/jokes that reach the heart.
- *Conscience*: use a story to set up the gospel point – *recognition of sin* or *remedy for sin* or *response to sin*. This is important, as it will give time for the laughter to settle. Do it too soon, and they will miss what you're saying.
- *Will*: a Bible verse to preach from, and then into the aspect of the gospel I am wanting to present to my hearers, ending with an appeal to the will to respond to the gospel.

My philosophy is 'pique the interest to preach the point', which I have illustrated below. The solid line represents the piquing of the hearer's interest. The three boxes with text are the preaching of the point and are parts of the gospel with Bible verses. The dashed lines represent the attention span of the hearer.

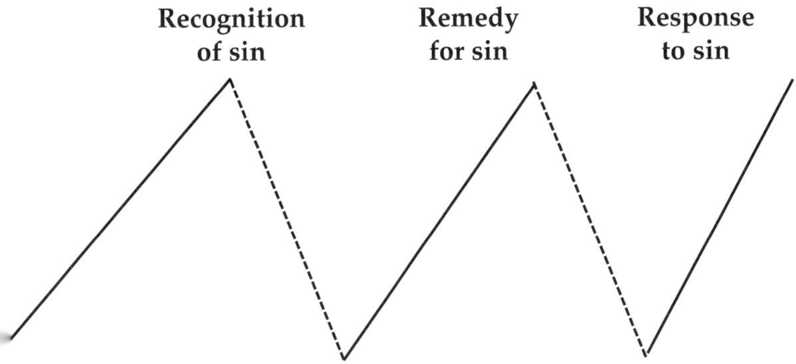

The piquing of the interest is more of a steady incline. This is because we should build slowly with our humour and narrative so we take our hearers with us. Once we have piqued the interest to preach the point, there is a sudden change of gear, whereby we go from making people *laugh* to making people *think* – we suddenly become serious. For this reason we need to understand that the attention and interest, as mentioned earlier in this chapter, will start to drop quite quickly – thus the steep decline as represented by the dashed line.

Precisely because this is what will happen, we need to be proactive. Two consecutive actions need to happen at this point. First: sharp, clear, non-religious preaching of the part of the gospel you are presenting, making reference to the other aspects. Second: we start the whole process again, piquing the interest to preach the point – and so back to the humour and the creative point.

7. Strike the balance

When I did my training in evangelism I was privileged to be sitting in a series of lectures on preaching by the brilliant and humorous communicator and evangelist,

Eric Delve. I remember him saying that constructing a sermon is like building a house. Among many things he commented on was the use of illustration. He talked of how illustrations were like windows. Too many, and the house is too light and without enough substance; but not enough illustration, and the house is dark and unattractive.

When we use humour, this is a great parallel. Too much humour, and there is no substance; too little humour, and it's unattractive. It's important to say at this point that this doesn't mean God won't use our talk if there's too much or too little humour. By the same token, let's not use that as an excuse not to sharpen up our communication.

I hope this chapter has been useful to you. Don't try to change everything at once but slowly make the changes so that you can become more creative in your presentation of the gospel.

My advice to you is simple: if you wish to sharpen your effectiveness as a communicator of the gospel – take humour seriously!

Chapter 5

All Roads Lead to God
Evangelism in an age of pluralism

Joseph Boot

> In teaching apologetics (the defense of the faith) and philosophy of religion for many years, we have found that students worry more and are embarrassed by Christianity's exclusivist claims than about any other aspect of their religion. In an age of toleration and pluralism, the most popular argument against the Christian religion seems to be simply that it is only one of many religions.
>
> *Handbook of Christian Apologetics: Hundreds of Answers to Crucial Questions* by Peter Kreeft and Ronald K. Tacelli (IVP, 1994).

Engaging other worldviews

It is noteworthy that St Peter, a man untrained in Greek philosophy, gives us the 'Magna Carta' of Christian apologetics in 1 Peter 3:15:

> But in your hearts set apart Christ as Lord. Always be prepared to give an answer to everyone who asks you to give the reason for the hope that you have (NIV).

The Greek word for 'answer' that Peter uses in this passage is *apologia*, from which we derive the term '*apologetics*'. The Greek word *logos* used for giving an 'account' or 'reason' is the word from which we derive our term 'logic'. The persecuted church is thus commissioned to give a logical and rational defence of the gospel whenever asked to do so. Equally important, St Paul tells us that his very ministry is defined by 'defending and confirming the gospel' (Phil. 1:7 NIV). Clearly, the task of explaining and justifying the Christian message over and against competing religious claims was a central concern to the apostles Peter and Paul, and indeed is evident in the whole biblical witness (cf. Jude 3). In reference to Peter's exhortation to give a *defence*, church historian Michael Haykin writes:

> The task of defending the Christian faith in the face of unbelief and the open rejection of biblical truth and the Christian world-view is a responsibility laid upon every generation of those who love the Lord Jesus Christ.[1]

In light of this mandate, it is important for all committed to sharing their faith to appreciate that the church in our day is facing serious challenges to its witness in terms of a philosophical and religious pluralism that has come to dominate Western culture. Despite the evident *fact* of Paul's standing before the Areopagus on Mars Hill in Acts 17 to defend the faith, or Peter in Acts 10 before the household of the Gentile Cornelius to proclaim Christ, contemporary Christian scholars feel forced to ask:

> Is it permissible for us Westerners and Christians still to talk about God as if our understanding of him is the only one possible? . . . Might it not be evidence of a higher universalism if we remained continually aware of our socio-cultural limitations and restrictions even in the field of religion?[2]

The common demarcation of Christian approaches to the status of non-Christian faiths and worldviews that face the believer today identifies three primary views: *exclusivism*, *inclusivism* and *pluralism*.

Pluralism

We are reminded on all sides that we now live in a pluralistic context and, as such, exclusivist claims about God and the way of salvation are out of place. For some humanistic scholars who still wear the garb of a Christian terminology but have emptied the faith of its true meaning, all religious claims are reduced to mythology and psychology in order to *escape history* and *abstract* a universal religion that acknowledges a nameless and mysterious divinity, or *ground of being*. Karen Armstrong writes, 'The various mythological stories, which were not intended to be taken literally, were an ancient form of psychology.'[3] These strange stories were 'bringing to light the obscure regions of the subconscious realm . . . because of the dearth of myth in our modern society we have had to evolve the science of psychoanalysis to help us deal with our inner world.'[4] For Armstrong, such myths as are found in the Bible only take on a semblance of 'reality' through ritual and mysticism that potentially lead to esoteric or 'intuitive insights'. God is removed from history and made a product of the subconscious mind. This leads to radical relativism and *pluralism* in understanding. So, to 'ask whether the Exodus from Egypt took place exactly as recounted in the Bible or to demand historical and scientific evidence to prove that it is factually true is to mistake the nature and purpose of this story'.[5] Its true purpose is apparently to inspire the mystical ritual of Passover as a rite of passage (like similar pagan rites) into a new reality! For Armstrong, such stories must be mythologized and 'liberated from the past'; this abstractionism paves the way for a fundamentalist *pluralism*. By ruling out a personal God who would make himself known in history, we discover a fatal bias of pluralists against the biblical traditions. Thus, as Vinoth Ramachandra observes, in the name of respect for 'diversity', the intellectual arrogance of pluralists

> savages [religious] pluralism in the name of defending it. What is put forward as a humble way of relating to the rich diversity of human religious traditions quickly turns into a reductionist onslaught on the factual affirmations of those traditions, with the Semitic traditions taking the brunt of the assault. What we are left with is a series of Procrustean beds on which a new elite of self-styled 'progressive' theologians dismember the religions of the world.[6]

It is very important to notice that Luke, the *careful historian*, writing the Book of Acts, notes both Peter's and Paul's insistence on the historical details of God's activity in history. This faith they proclaimed was not viewed as a product of their subconscious, a myth of the imagination, but as concrete historical reality to which they were witnesses (Acts 10:37–41; 17:26,31–32). Just as some of the Athenians sneered at the claimed historical, physical resurrection of Christ because of their Greek philosophical dualism,[7] so today the historical claims of the Christian faith militate against contemporary pluralism. As the radical 'Christian' pluralist John Hick admits:

> There is a direct line of logical entailment from the premise that Jesus was God, in the sense that he was God the

> Son, the second person of the Divine Trinity, living in a human life, to the conclusion that Christianity, and Christianity alone, was founded by God in person; and from this to the further conclusion that God must want all his human children to be related to him through his religion which he has himself founded for us; and then to the final conclusion, 'Outside Christianity, no salvation'.[8]

Consequently, *exclusivist* views are unpalatable to many 'Christians', so it is not uncommon to hear pluralists speak with admiration of Gandhi's or the Dali Lama's faith perspectives. Catholic theologian Hans Kung notes:

> In one way or another, many Europeans and Americans would subscribe to Gandhi's words: 'I believe in the Bible as I believe in the Gita. I regard all the great faiths of the world as equally true with my own . . .'[9]

Thus *pluralism* is essentially the view that no religion can make the claim to absolute uniqueness. Not only are there many ways to salvation through Jesus, but Jesus is only one means of salvation among many – a path among many paths amid the world's religions. As such, to share one's faith with the goal of bringing about conversion would be seen as immoral. The consequences of such a view are clear: Peter's address to Cornelius and Paul's apologetic to the Athenians in the Book of Acts were both unethical forms of violence. Ajith Fernando observes:

> A direct result of such thinking is that apologetics – defending the truthfulness of one's beliefs against opposing views – is considered undesirable and in need of replacement by dialogue. But dialogue here has the aim of mutual enrichment, not conversion.[10]

As we look at two apologetic engagements by the apostles, we will see that neither Peter nor Paul were engaged in an ecumenical, inter-faith dialogue seeking 'personal enrichment' from humanism and paganism – both were proclaiming the faith with the object of bringing their hearers to faith in Christ. It is therefore difficult to see how pluralism can be seen as Christian in origin at all – for as Ronald Nash notes, 'When people adopt pluralism, they must abandon every core doctrine of the Christian faith'.[11] By the very fact of their inter-faith engagements and efforts at conversion, it is obvious from Scripture that Peter and Paul were operating on assumptions opposite to those of pluralism.

Inclusivism

This view seeks to retain the doctrine that salvation is available only through Christ, but widens the means by which it may be appropriated by the individual. Nobody can be saved apart from Christ, whatever religion they may follow, say inclusivists, but, given that multitudes of people have not and will not hear a direct proclamation of the gospel in their lifetime, it would seem *more just* of God to provide access to Christ's redemptive work through the illumination they may be sincerely seeking by their own religious faiths, practices and devotion. That is, for people pursuing a life of peace, reconciliation and justice, God's saving grace is *already* shown to be at work in their lives. As a consequence, Christ's uniqueness is not denied but his work is defined differently. Inclusivists often make a distinction between the *ontological* necessity of Christ's saving work (its actual reality) and the differing claim concerning knowledge of that work as *epistemologically* necessary (it being consciously known). What this means is that Christ's redemptive work is seen as a necessary *ground* for people to be saved, but *knowledge* of Christ or *belief* in Christ are not necessary for those of other faiths and worldviews to enjoy the benefits of his atonement.

For many, the attractiveness of the inclusivist view lies in the argument that it would surely be *unfair* of God to ordain the need for *conscious knowledge* of Christ and belief in his redemptive work as a *precondition* of salvation, since access to such knowledge is clearly not based on an egalitarian framework – not everyone has the same access to Christian truth. This was an argument urged by primitive pagan critics of the early church's theology, such as Porphyry (232–303 CE) and Julian the Apostate (332–63 CE).[12]

Inclusivism is therefore increasingly popular in contemporary Christianity, often being carried to the extent that full salvation is seen as extended to those *actively hostile* to Christ and opposed to his deity, redemption and lordship, so long as certain conditions of goodness and sincerity are met. For example, Samir Selmanovic, a pastor and part of the coordinating group for the 'evangelical' 'Emergent Village', tells of his non-Christian friend Mark in New York who stated that 'to become a part of Christianity would be a moral step backwards',[13] but who nonetheless senses transcendence to his existence, believing it to be a gift, turning to this 'grace' in his *inner life* and granting himself a new beginning. Though rejecting Christianity, Mark seeks to be a channel of good to others.[14]

Selmanovic writes that this unbeliever's opinion 'embodies the doctrine of creation, sin, salvation, and new life. That's Christ, embedded in the life of Mark, present in substance rather than in name.'[15] We shall see whether Peter's or Paul's approach to evangelism and apologetics supports such a view.

Exclusivism

The Christian philosopher Ronald Nash summarizes well the exclusivist view as it relates to both to inclusivism and pluralism:

> Christian exclusivism can be defined as the belief that (1) Jesus Christ is the only saviour, and (2) explicit faith in Jesus Christ is necessary for salvation. The first claim denies that there are or can be other saviours, a fact that distinguishes it from pluralism. The second claim denies that people may be saved without conscious and explicit faith in Jesus Christ, which sets it apart from inclusivism.[16]

Consequently, for the exclusivist, beliefs logically incompatible with revealed Christianity are false and cannot be 'saving'. God alone is the author of salvation and no form of human effort, goodwill or merit can place us in right standing with God without the revelation of Christ and explicit faith in him. For those people truly responding to the *general revelation* of God in creation and conscience, drawn by his grace, *God will send* further revelation, so that faith in his name and work is made possible. Infants who die without reaching an age of comprehension and those mentally handicapped whose judgement is impaired are left in the just and merciful hands of God.

Models of biblical apologetics in a pluralistic culture

1. The audience

We have seen, then, that the *fact* of the apostles' engagement with non-Christian worldviews mandates us to do the same. Apologetics is relevant! However, the evangelistic approach of both Paul and Peter is dramatically shaped by the people to whom their message is to be addressed. This is a crucial lesson for us as we seek to engage with diverse people and views present in contemporary culture.

In the classic New Testament model of biblical apologetics (Acts 17:16–34), Paul is confronted by a profoundly challenging context in which to proclaim Christ. His spirit being provoked by a city full of idols (verse 16), he first speaks with Jews and God-fearing Gentiles and then finds himself conversing with Epicurean and Stoic philosophers in the market-place. His discussion themes being Christ and the resurrection, his opponents are not friendly, referring to him as, literally, a 'seed-picker', a kind of pseudo-intellectual who had picked up odd ideas here and there without coherence (verse 18). Nonetheless, they invite him to address the intellectual court of the Areopagus, probably in order to see if he should be granted a public licence for lecturing.

Athens was the philosophical centre of the ancient world. As part of the Roman Empire, it was characterized by large-scale philosophical pluralism and state-sponsored religious pluralism. It was home to four prestigious schools of thought: the 'Academy' of Plato, the Lyceum of Aristotle, the Garden of Epicurus and the Painted Porch of Zeno, all dating from around 300 BC.[17] Paul found himself addressing the disciples of Epicurus and Zeno.

The Epicureans were ancient naturalists (atomists) who held that a naturalistic explanation for all events must be given – not unlike the popular atheist propagandist from Oxford, Richard Dawkins. With lasting pleasure as the goal of existence in this life alone, transcendent purpose and reality was denied – once you are dead, your atoms simply disperse into infinite space.

Zeno, the founder of the Stoic school, agreed with the Epicureans in holding that the senses alone can provide knowledge and that the mind is like a blank sheet of paper at birth. However, he exalted *reason*, rather than chance, as governing all matter. The highest expression of nature was reason or world-soul finally personified as god. His view of history as moving in great circles precluded personal immortality for the individual.[18] Since human beings were subordinate to this historical determinism (fatalism), the only way to live was to live in harmony with nature, the highest expression of which is reason, so one should suppress the emotional element.

In Paul's day, the intellectual climate was one of uncertainty and turmoil – scepticism was the order of the day. The Christian apologist Greg Bahnsen notes:

> over four hundred years of philosophical dispute with its conflicts, repetitions, and inadequacies had left many Athenians bored and thirsty for novel schemes of thought. Thus one can understand Luke's accurate and insightful aside to the readers in Acts 17:21, 'now all the Athenians and the strangers sojourning there spent time in nothing else, but either to tell or to hear some new thing'.[19]

We are then in good company, for Paul is confronted with intellectual arrogance, radical pluralism and biblical illiteracy more than rivalling our own current context.

Peter's audience in Acts 10:1–48, beyond the fact that they were also Gentile, was in stark contrast to Paul's in Acts 17. After his extraordinary vision and preparation, Peter finds himself in the Gentile city of Caesarea, in the home of a Roman centurion. Centurions in the New Testament make frequent and favourable appearances. The first Gentile that we know of who had dealings with Jesus was also a centurion, stationed in Capernaum (Luke 7:2–10; Matt. 8:5–13). Cornelius was prepared for his encounter with Peter by a visionary experience. Cornelius is important because, like many that we still encounter in the West, he was a 'God-fearer'. F. F. Bruce remarks:

> Many Gentiles of those days, while not prepared to become full converts to Judaism (the requirement of circumcision being a special stumbling block for them), were attracted by the simple monotheism of Jewish synagogue worship and by the ethical standards of a Jewish way of life. Some of them attended synagogue and became tolerably conversant with the prayers and scripture lessons . . .[20]

As a hang-over from a long Christian past, we still encounter people on the fringes of the church and faith who hold broadly theistic assumptions and even periodically attend worship services – especially at Christmas and Easter. Luke tells us that Cornelius regularly prayed to Yahweh and did acts of mercy and charity for the people of Israel. This response to God had 'come up as a memorial offering before God' (Acts 10:4 NIV). Thus, Peter was addressing a man in a similar condition to some of those worshippers gathered on the day of Pentecost (Acts 2:9–12) or the Ethiopian eunuch reading the prophet Isaiah, led to faith in

Christ by Phillip the evangelist (Acts 8:26–39). Cornelius was a man who acknowledged the God of Israel in prayer, knew something of the Scriptures, and was concerned to show mercy. As Bruce notes, 'Never had a preacher of the gospel a more promising audience.'[21] The contrast, then, between the house of Cornelius and the court of the Areopagus could not be greater. Both of these groups of people are present in our time.

2. *The messenger*

The respective apologetic approaches of Paul and Peter were not only shaped by the audience, but were the product of their divine preparation by birth, experience, education and miraculous calling. Paul was a Jew and a citizen of Tarsus, a significant metropolis. Famed as a city of great learning, it was noted for schools devoted to philosophy and rhetoric. The great Stoic leaders Zeno, Antipater, Heraclides and Athenodoras the Stoic all hailed from Paul's own city. It is likely that Tarsus exercised considerable academic influence on Paul. He was an exceptionally gifted student (Gal. 1:14) and studied under Gamaliel (Acts 22:3) in Jerusalem. Bahnsen notes the significance of this for his encounter at the Areopagus:

> His course of study would have included critical courses in Greek culture and philosophy (as evidence from the Talmud indicates). When we add to this the extensive knowledge of Greek literature and culture which is reflected in his letters it is manifest that Paul was neither naïve nor obscurantist when it came to a knowledge of philosophy and Gentile thought. Given his background, training, and expertise in scriptural theology, Paul was

> the ideal representative for the classic confrontation of Jerusalem with Athens.[22]

Furthermore, though the encounter in Acts 17 is not directly preceded by revelation in a vision (as in Peter's case in Acts 10), Paul *already knew* his calling to the Gentile world through a vision of his own. He knew that he had been sent and that the gospel promises were extended to them in Christ (Acts 13:46–49). The very conversion of St Paul was a sovereign act of God, selecting him as his *chosen instrument* for preaching to the Gentiles (Acts 9:15). When Paul stood before the Areopagus in Athens, he doubtless recalled the words he had heard from heaven on the road to Damascus as Christ commissioned him to go to the Gentiles and 'open their eyes and turn them from darkness to light, and from the power of Satan to God, so that they may receive forgiveness of sins and a place among those who are sanctified by faith in me' (Acts 26:18 NIV). In light of such a statement, there can be little doubt that the assumptions of contemporary religious pluralism and inclusivism did not even enter Paul's mind as he addressed himself to the Athenian court.

St Peter's preparation was equally miraculous, though as a man he was very different from Paul. He was, likewise, a first-century Jew, but a peasant. Despite a miraculous calling away from his vocation as a fisherman to become a 'fisher of men', walking with Christ for three years, hearing the Great Commission (Matt. 28:18–20), seeing God move among non-Jews at Pentecost (Acts 2:1ff) and doubtless hearing of the Ethiopian eunuch's conversion (Acts 8:26–39), he was still wrestling with various scruples about the universality of the gospel. His preparation was privileged and extensive, but since he was a Jew and a devout follower of the law, a monumental shift needed to take place in his thinking. To enter a Gentile's house and accept the hospitality of that house was to be rendered ceremonially unclean; it was therefore necessary for Peter to understand that the ceremonial aspects of the law, that were illustrative shadows, had now been set aside. This realization appears to have come much more easily to Paul (from his conversion), who later had to reprimand Peter for his practical, if not theological, inconsistency in this matter (Gal. 2:11–21).

Peter's vision of the sheet filled with quadrupeds, reptiles and birds, together with the voice from heaven commanding him to 'kill and eat', began a revolution in his thinking. His initial response, protesting that he had never touched unclean things (Acts 10:14), is met with the assurance that God has cleansed these things, so that they should no longer be considered unholy (Acts 10:15). This happens three times, and as he ponders the meaning of the vision, a messenger from Cornelius' house arrives. The significance of the vision soon becomes clear to him – God has taught him to call no *human being* profane or unclean (Acts 10:28). This was monumental! As Ramachandra rightly points out:

> Here we are introduced to a stupendous sight, unimaginable in the ancient world, of a Jewish peasant under the same roof as a Roman military officer . . . Peter, witnessing the same Holy Spirit at work in the Gentile's life, comes to a recognition of his own cultural prejudice under the deepening impact of the gospel on his thinking. Cornelius has come to a saving knowledge of Christ. Peter has come to a deeper discipleship . . .[23]

God's preparation of his messenger shaped Peter's evangelistic approach 'as he went'. By contrast, Paul's conversion experience and early travels among pagans had already developed his thinking before he reached Athens. But Peter, as he encountered Cornelius, was being broadened to recognize that the God of Israel was never a tribal God, of one nation, but the God of all peoples. A national God was the invention of later Jewish imagination, not the God of Abraham, who promised that through his seed all the nations of the world would be blessed (Gen. 12:3). Suddenly, at the house of Cornelius, as the Holy Spirit descends, Peter is aware that God is no respecter of persons (Acts 10:34–35). Peter could be said to have been *taught* an apologetic approach in this incident that was to shape and transform his thinking for the future.

We see, then, that both Paul and Peter as *messengers* were prepared for these encounters so that just as character and plot can never be separated, so evangelistic *method* and *messenger* cannot be divorced. Both of these engagements reveal that God prepares and conditions our lives in every way to fit us to reach those in our spheres of influence. In an important sense the messenger embodies and incarnates the method, so that God uses our whole being, background, family, education, proclivities and personalities as well as his miraculous interventions to mould our engagements with the non-believer. Moreover, there are times when our encounters with non-believers serve to help us better comprehend the gospel message and further disclose its distinctiveness.

Message and method

1. Paul in Athens

Paul's whole posture in Athens clearly decimates the pluralist perspective. We read in this text a rational defence of the gospel combined with a critique of the opponents' worldview. Paul's approach is characterized by what we call 'Christian apologetics'. The gospel and apologetics cannot be artificially divorced. As Alister McGrath says, 'The New Testament brings the two together in a creative and productive interplay: to proclaim the gospel is to defend the gospel, just as to defend the gospel is to proclaim the gospel.'[24]

What prompted this encounter is important. Paul is waiting in Athens for his companions and, far from being impressed by Athenian culture, aesthetics and religious insights, hoping to be personally enriched in a 'learning experience' with paganism, his spirit is *provoked* within him. The Greek word translated as 'provoked' or 'greatly distressed' (Acts 17:16 NIV) is the same word used in the Greek Old Testament for God's anger at Israel's *idolatry*. Don Carson rightly notes that 'The New Testament writers did not readily distinguish the pluralism of the day from the idolatry of the day: the destruction of the one was the destruction of the other.'[25] Paul would have seen images of Neptune and Bacchus and the forty-foot-high statue of Athena, the goddess of the city – the city literally teemed with idols. Deeply distressed by this, he began by *discussing* and *reasoning* in the synagogue and then in the market-place with whomever was present. Paul's method was eminently appropriate to the context. Bahnsen states:

> The Greek word for Paul's activity recalls the 'dialogues' of Plato wherein Socrates discusses issues of philosophical importance; it is the same word used by Plutarch for the teaching methods of a peripatetic philosopher. Paul did not simply announce his viewpoint; he discussed it openly and gave it a reasonable defense. He aimed to educate his audience, not to make common religious cause with their sinful ignorance.[26]

As Paul shares the *gospel of Christ*, his philosophically sophisticated hearers mistakenly consider him to be proclaiming a strange new divine couple: 'Jesus' (a masculine form) and the 'resurrection' (a feminine form), personifying powers of healing and restoration. This gospel proclamation was sufficient to have Paul hauled before the Areopagus (literally 'Mars Hill') council. This council played an important part in Athenian life. Cicero tells us that the Areopagus assembly governed Athenian affairs of state – its jurisdiction and responsibilities were both religious and civil.[27] So, picture the scene. Paul, now before the court, is accused of teaching about 'strange deities' or 'foreign gods' (Acts 17:18 NIV) in the same city in which Anaxagoras, Socrates and Protagoras had been tried for introducing new deities.

Paul is here confronted with the total pagan – people who have never read the Old Testament, know nothing of the messianic prophecies, are not proselytes to Judaism nor God-fearers like Cornelius. Consequently, of necessity, *his approach*, like our own among biblical illiterates and modern pagans, must be different from Peter's in Acts 10 and even his own approach in places like Antioch (Acts 13:13ff). The Epicureans were materialists and the Stoics pantheists. Their monistic philosophies, by definition, denied the infinite personal Creator God of Scripture. Their use of the term *God* was a limiting concept – little more than the deification of human reason or natural forces. It is interesting, then, that Paul's method does not begin with an attempted classical 'proof' of the existence of God (theism), so common in modern Christian apologetics. Paul recognizes that such proofs are largely redundant because men and women *know* that they are creatures of the living God but suppress this truth in unrighteousness (Rom. 1:18–20). This knowledge is so evident that they are without *apologia* (defence) for their sinful rejection of him (Rom. 1:20). Paul is confident as he embarks on his defence that he can take this fact for granted:

> Paul does not prove that God exists and is actually known by men. But, like the whole of the Old and New Testaments and incidentally the whole catholic tradition and also (unlike Barth) the Reformers, he takes these things for granted.[28]

Though bold, Paul is *not arrogant* in his approach. He begins with courtesy and respect but with no indication of viewing their religion as an alternative way of salvation (Acts 17:22). On the contrary, his mission to the 'wisdom lovers' of Athens afforded him further confirmation of what he already knew – that 'in the wisdom of God the world through its wisdom did not know him' (1 Cor. 1:21 NIV).[29]

Although the specific question the Athenian intellectuals asked was about the resurrection, he begins his address by identifying the true and living God; there is, interestingly, no suggestion that Paul rallies various evidential arguments to bolster the claim of the resurrection. Instead of starting with this isolated fact, which would have been seen as a monstrous story about a resuscitated corpse and thereby a meaningless occurrence, he lays the presuppositional groundwork so that the resurrection can later be interpreted in its proper framework. Paul clearly realizes that between him and his hearers lies a total conflict in systems of thought. This is very different from Peter's situation when addressing Cornelius. In that instance the hearers share essentially the same theological assumptions, so only more revelation of the *same kind* is required. Here in Athens a total intellectual and spiritual reorientation is needed.

Paul's strategy is to first identify a *point of contact* by exposing the perverted and suppressed knowledge of the true God found in inscriptions on the altar(s) in the city: 'To an Unknown God.' What Paul does here is reinforce their self-confessed religious ignorance represented in their practices, which he later underscores as idolatry for which repentance is required. He is evidently *not* establishing a 'natural theology' to argue from rationalistic 'first principles' like a pagan philosopher, but is seeking to confront them with their sinful pride. There is a striking similarity of theme here, though the tone is different, to his discussion in Romans 1 – 3. F. F. Bruce helps us here:

> The knowledge of God, according to Paul in Romans 1:19–22, *was accessible to all in his works of creation, but the capacity or desire to acquire it had been impaired by idolatry*. If the author of Romans 1 – 3 had been invited to address an Athenian audience on the knowledge of God, it is difficult to see how the general purport of his words could have been much different from what Luke here reports Paul as saying. The tone of the Areopagitica is different from that of Romans 1 – 3, but Paul knew the wisdom of adapting his tone and general approach to the particular audience or readership being addressed at the time [*emphasis mine*].[30]

These factors militate strongly against Alister McGrath's view that

> Paul is able to *base himself* upon *acceptable Greek theistic assumptions*, while at the same time going beyond them. Paul shows a clear appreciation of the apologetic potential of stoic philosophy, portraying the gospel as resonating with central stoic concerns, while extending the limits of what might be known [*emphasis mine*].[31]

While the gospel clearly does deal effectively with human concerns, McGrath's view appears mistaken. First, Stoics were not *theists* in anything resembling a biblical sense, but pantheists. Second, Paul gives no indication in our text that their *assumptions* are *acceptable* – quite the contrary. The message of Romans 1 and Acts 17 does not reveal a basic compatibility of the biblical worldview with Greek philosophy but establishes it as the very antithesis of paganism. Third, Paul is not merely trying to 'extend the limits' of pagan thought as though it were right as far as it went, simply requiring some additional information to be complete – rather, he challenges its very foundational assumptions as distortion of truth. They have mishandled God's general revelation and become fools (cf. Rom. 1:21–22).[32] But the point of contact is not lost; it is in the fact that as creatures of God, men and women cannot escape the knowledge of God. Even in their rebellious philosophies that worship the creature or mysterious forces rather than the Creator, their culpability is betrayed by their tacit acknowledgement of the truths they have suppressed. As Bahnsen puts it, 'Paul was noting the basic schizophrenia in unbelieving thought when he described in the Athenians both an awareness of God (verse 22) and an ignorance of God (verse 23).'[33]

Having established the point of contact, Paul goes on to assert the biblical doctrine of God and of creation – he educates his listeners with a biblical worldview (Acts 17:24–25). Although he is not directly quoting from the Old Testament, there is no mistaking its origin in Scripture: 'His argument is firmly based on biblical revelation; it echoes throughout the thought, and at times the very language, of the Old Testament. Like the biblical revelation itself, his argument begins with God the creator of all and ends with God the judge of all.'[34] In verse 26 Paul speaks of a God who is sovereign over all of history – not only does he create and judge but he governs all things by his sovereign determination from the first man to the very boundaries of human empire. Events and history are not random but are ordered so that people will seek after God (Acts 17:27); this goodness of God should lead people to repentance (cf. Rom. 2:4).

This worldview strongly militated against the Epicurean and Stoic view of the divine. For the Epicurean, the gods were made of very fine atoms and so lived in tranquillity in the spaces between the worlds – they were not involved in the concrete facts of human history. *God* for the Stoics was an all-pervasive impersonal principle of reason. Over and against such views, Paul presents the God of Scripture as a transcendent yet personal God, distinct from his creation, governing all things and bringing all into judgement. Paul contrasts divine will and sovereignty with human dependence and need. The pagan view of cyclic history is firmly refuted in terms of the doctrines of creation and providence and final judgement (Acts 17:31).

Paul continues his argument by quoting some of their *own pagan sources* to further manifest their guilt. Despite God's drawing people to seek him, due to sin, they grope about for him, even though he is not far from us (Acts 17:27). Paul reveals that, by virtue of being God's creatures, even pantheistic Stoics are aware of this. He cites Epimenides the Cretan from a quatrain in an address to Zeus, 'in him we live and move and have our being' (Acts 17:28 NIV), which is reminiscent of Paul's statement in Colossians 1:15–17. Paul uses this quote to emphasize the *total dependence* of people upon God for their existence. The second statement, 'for we also are his offspring', is quoted from his fellow Cilician, Aratus, in a poem on 'Natural Phenomena' (echoed also in Cleanthes' 'Hymn to Zeus').[35] In light of the pluralistic thinking of our time, it is important to see what Paul is and is not saying here. Is he commending Stoic doctrines or reducing Christian categories to Greek philosophy? Is this an inclusivist 'preparation of grace' whereby the Athenians are already sincerely on their way to a true knowledge of God? F. F. Bruce thinks not:

> In both these poems Zeus is considered . . . as the supreme being of Greek and especially Stoic philosophy. But did Paul intend to identify the Zeus of Greek philosophy *simpliciter* with the God of biblical revelation, whom in his letters he repeatedly calls 'the God and Father of our Lord Jesus Christ'? Quite certainly not.[36]

Equally, Paul is not simply equivocating with pantheistic terms and using the quotes out of context and applying a totally foreign biblically theistic meaning. *Truly* we are God's offspring, but not in the pantheistic sense of Aratus – Paul has *already defined* the God of which he speaks. So, Paul is not *employing* pagan ideas here; rather, as Bahnsen says, he is using 'pagan expressions to demonstrate that ungodly pagan thinkers have not eradicated all idea, albeit suppressed and distorted, of the living and true God'.[37] F. F. Bruce agrees, saying, 'The delicately suited allusions to Stoic and Epicurean tenets . . . have their place as points of contact with the audience, but they do not commit the speaker to acquiescence in the realm of ideas to which they originally belong.'[38]

Finally, Paul's typically Jewish polemic culminates in admonition and a call to repentance. Paul has argued that God cannot be a graven image, the handiwork of a craftsman. A further statement against idolatry (Acts 17:29) is followed by recognition of God's mercy in overlooking this ignorance, and so now he calls *all everywhere* to repent (Acts 17:30). As Bruce says, 'if ignorance of the divine nature was culpable before, it is inexcusable now'.[39] The important point to notice here is that the all-encompassing nature of this call *destroys pluralism*. If many religious paths lead to the same God, as pluralists claim, then there is certainly no need for such rational, educated and morally sensitive philosophers to turn to Christ – Mars Hill, for such thinkers, is a futile and pointless engagement! Equally important, why should Paul have stressed repentance and turning to the judge of the earth so greatly if the citations from the poets actually inferred that these pagans were reaching for the living God in god-honouring sincerity through their own traditions?

Here the inclusivist (based on his or her own definitions) is forced to acknowledge, due to the reality of Christ's atoning death and the 'sincerity' and 'moral life' of the Stoic, that these philosophers were better off *before* Paul preached to them. Since, for the inclusivist, the salvation of Christ may be extended to all people sincerely seeking God within their own religious contexts without explicit knowledge of Christ, why interfere, pressing people for conversion? Exposing the Athenians to a gospel proclamation only served to *condemn* the majority that did not turn to Christ. It seems then that the inclusivist view forces us to say that Paul should have left off his discourse in verse 28, or better still, not addressed these well-meaning philosophers at all. Ironically, the preaching of the gospel for the inclusivist may actually serve to accomplish the exact opposite of his desired ends – condemnation rather than inclusion for the 'sincere' heathen. In the end it is doubtful that the Paul of Acts 17 and Romans 1 – 3 recognized any such category of 'sincere' unbeliever (cf. Rom. 1:28–32; 3:9–19; Acts 17:30).

The conclusion of Paul's address focuses on the coming judgement and Christ's resurrection as its proof. He has reasoned implicitly (not explicitly) from the Old Testament Scriptures, beginning with the Creator of all and concluding with the Judge of all! He did not ask the Athenians to adjust or refine their thinking a little, but called for total change. Here Paul introduces the 'Son of Man' eschatology of the Gospels (Acts 17:31). God has given to a true man authority to execute judgement (cf. John 5:27). Paul has not departed from the apostolic witness, for the resurrection is cited as the event which establishes this claim. The ridicule that follows the statement about the resurrection is rooted in the familiar facet of neo-Platonic dualism. The physical world being bad or evil and the spiritual world being good, why would a good God wish to raise a physical being to life? But despite some sneering, others wanted to hear him again on the subject, and others 'joined him' and became believers (two are named – a man and a woman – plus a group of others, the number of whom is not mentioned). F. F. Bruce notes that the speech 'admirably summarizes an introductory lesson in Christianity for cultured pagans . . . the essential content of the speech is biblical, but the presentation is Hellenistic'.[40]

Paul's apologetic method, which destroys pluralism and strongly questions the assumptions of inclusivism, is clearly seen to be one of *apologetic confrontation* between 'Jerusalem and Athens', Hebraic in content but Hellenistic (Greek) in presentation. Setting an example for us to follow, he sets out an entire worldview, *educating* his opponents before introducing them to the Son of Man and the resurrection. His method never assumed a 'neutral' stance but rather emphasized the antithesis between himself and paganism. Yet this did not eliminate the point of contact with the non-believer found in our *common creation in the image of God* and his self-revelation in nature and history – the suppression of this revelation forming the basis of Paul's appeal to repent from idolatry and turn to God, our righteous judge. Bahnsen summarizes for us: 'The Apostles' apologetical method for reasoning with educated unbelievers who did not acknowledge scriptural authority turns out to be a suitable pattern for our defending the faith today.'[41]

2. *Peter and Cornelius*

By contrast, in the Acts 10 account, both parties have been prepared by a vision for the encounter. Peter's message and method was a tried and tested one, a classic example of the apostolic witness that mirrors previous addresses to God-fearing Gentiles in Acts 2 and Jews in Acts 4 and 5. The contrast in approach is most striking, but it is equally important to note some commonalities in content. As Bruce notes, Peter begins with a highly significant statement 'sweeping away the racial and religious prejudices of centuries'.[42] For a Jew to say that God does not show partiality (Acts 10:34) and to universalize the message to every nation was no small matter. This resonates with the same demolition of racial prejudice found in Paul (Acts 17:26–29). Both recognized that God's choice of Israel was an act of grace and that the sovereign ordering of history was so that people would seek him. This should not have been new to Peter, since this fact was embedded in the prophets (cf. Isa. 19:25). Peter also begins with an emphasis on the lordship of Christ (Acts 10:36). Again, this is similar to Paul's affirmation in Acts 17:25. In verse 40 Peter's words turn to the resurrection of Christ and, like Paul in Acts 17:31, he immediately applies this historical reality to God's appointment of Christ to be the judge of the living and the dead (Acts 10:42). In both addresses, then, we have an affirmation of the universality of God's call in the gospel. We have the concept of lordship attributed to the triune God and the proclamation of the resurrection as proof of a final judgement through God's appointed man – Christ Jesus. Here the similarities end. What fills the gaps distinguishes the evangelistic approach of each – necessary in order to address the particular audience with which they were confronted.

The critical phrase is found in verse 37: 'You know what has happened throughout Judea, beginning in Galilee' (NIV). Peter's entire address assumes not only a prior acquaintance with the Hebrew Scriptures (Acts 10:43) but a specific knowledge of the immediate events in the life, ministry and death of Christ (Acts 10:37–39). This is not unlike many today who have had some background in the church, or whose parents were churchgoers, or whose religious studies in school have given them some acquaintance with the life of Christ. Peter's message is essentially a summary of typical apostolic preaching covering events from John's baptism to the resurrection and judgement. Actually, the scope of the address mirrors that of Mark's Gospel. Obviously the total ignorance of the pagans in Acts 17 of both Scripture and the historical details of Jesus' ministry made such an approach for Paul impossible. The power of Peter's discourse lay, then, in his ability to proclaim Christ as God's 'anointed' (Acts 10:38), literally God's Messiah (*Christos*), foretold by the prophets (Acts 10:43). Since they were God-fearing adherents to Judaism, these terms would have been comprehensible and meaningful to the household of Cornelius.

The unanticipated element in this for Peter was the fact of the sovereign descent of the Holy Spirit upon those listening to the message (Acts 10:44). The speaking with tongues certainly convinced him finally that God was accepting Gentiles and water baptism could not be refused them (Acts 10:47; 11:17). But why did the Spirit not fall in the same way on the Areopagus at Mars Hill? God's ways are not our ways (Isa. 55:8). Perhaps in terms of God's covenant, Cornelius' entire household was receiving a corporate work of grace that could not be bestowed upon a crowd of sneering philosophers (Acts 17:32). Further, it is doubtful that the pagans, not knowing the Scriptures, would have understood the significance of the pouring out of God's Spirit (Joel 2:28–29). Equally, it seems the gift of tongues was as much a sign for Peter and his companions, confirming the acceptance of Gentiles by God, as it was a sign for Cornelius' household (Acts 11:17–18).

Peter's encounter with Cornelius is a passage favoured by many inclusivists, believing that in it they find support for their position (particularly Acts 10:34–35). J. Andrew Kirk says: 'Cornelius stands for all God-fearing people who, because they pray to God regularly and give generously to those in need, are accepted by him.'[43] Clearly, Cornelius believed in Yahweh and was consequently in a similar position spiritually to a believing Jew of the time. But how does this support inclusivism? Ronald Nash writes:

> The entire story is supposed to support the inclusivist distinction between believers and Christians. According to John Saunders, 'Cornelius was already a saved believer before Peter arrived but he was not a Christian believer.'[44]

Is this isolated statement from verse 35 really sufficient to support the notion that those who believe in a supreme being and try to live a good life are acceptable to God? Can we approach the Father without the Son, as increasing numbers of 'evangelicals' claim (John 14:6; 1 John 2:23)? The Pelagian assumption that good works can make one acceptable to God seems equally erroneous in light of biblical teaching (cf. Rom. 3:9–20). The inclusivist criterion would mean all theistic Jews and Gentiles at the time of Christ and since are saved. Clark Pinnock describes Cornelius as 'the pagan saint par excellence of the New Testament'[45] and in the same light sees Paul's address in Acts 17:28 as an approving nod to pagan thinking.[46]

What, then, is the point of the apologetics and preaching to them? Clearly there is fuzzy thinking here. Scripture is clear that Jews in the Old Testament were *not saved* through 'good works' and believing in the existence of Yahweh, but by faithful obedience to the covenant expressed through the Law and sacrificial system that foreshadowed the atoning death of Christ. Scripture is categorical that only those who put faith in and *welcomed the promises*, joining faith in those promises to obedience, were saved before Christ (cf. John 8:56; Heb. 11:13–16); multitudes of 'believing' Jews perished in the desert and in Korah's rebellion (Jude 5–11). The *promises to be believed* concerned Christ's coming and his saving work. Our Lord himself condemns believing (theistic) Jews who do not believe *in him* as the *fulfilment* of those promises (cf. John 8:31–39). Nicodemus was clearly a God-fearing believer who even recognized the hand of God in our Lord's teaching, and yet Jesus told him he needed to be 'born again', without which he could not see the kingdom of God (John 3:3).

Critically, the Acts 10 passage itself refutes the inclusivist viewpoint. Peter reports Cornelius' own testimony: 'Send to Joppa for Simon who is called Peter. He will bring you a message through which you and all your household will be saved' (Acts 11:13–14 NIV). This is the same Greek word used for our salvation in Christ and our deliverance by God. Clearly Cornelius believed the angel and recognized that he was not yet 'saved'. At the conclusion of Peter's report to the apostles and leaders in Jerusalem, they glorify God for the salvation of Cornelius' household, saying, 'So then, God has granted even the Gentiles repentance unto life' (Acts 11:18 NIV). This clearly implies that prior to this, Cornelius had not experienced *repentance that leads to life*. It therefore seems obvious that far from supporting inclusivism, this account strongly undermines it. Inclusivism appears to be an emotive romantic project, not a biblical teaching. It rests on out-of-context proof texts and *speculations* that are not authorized by Scripture (cf. Deut. 29:29). Just as Paul and Peter trusted God to be the judge of the unbeliever, so should we (cf. Gen. 18:25). The kind of populist teaching propounded by Clark Pinnock, which holds that hostile atheists who nonetheless 'love' their neighbour have in fact responded positively to God despite their protestations to the contrary, is surely indulgence in wishful thinking.[47]

Conclusions

The entire Book of Acts witnesses against both pluralism and inclusivism. Only by removing the *atonement* and *resurrection* of Christ to practical irrelevance (central components of both Acts 10 and 17) can the pluralistic or inclusivist model stand. Paul (Saul) himself certainly would have passed the tests for inclusivist salvation before turning to Christ; but clearly his zeal for the God of Israel was not enough.

Peter and Paul's evangelistic approaches were both eminently fitted to the occasion – faithful to the apostolic witness, Hebraic in content, and with Paul, Greek in method. Both encounters seriously undermine the claims of both pluralism and inclusivism. The lessons for our time are clear.

First, we should not forget that, as Ramachandra says, 'the Christian movement was born into a world every bit as pluralistic in ideology and behavior as our own'.[48] Consequently Acts remains the Christian model in apologetic approach to inter-faith engagement.

Second, this model involves uncompromising faithfulness to the doctrines of the gospel laid down in Mark's Gospel (as well as the other Gospels) that is found in outline form in Peter's address to Cornelius.

Third, when dealing with the biblically illiterate non-believer, we must cultivate the skill of St Paul, who presented the Christian faith as a full-orbed worldview, educating and persuading his disputants in terms of Christian presuppositions so that the critical events like the resurrection could be *interpreted* in the proper light.

Fourth, we must learn to defend the faith as the Scripture itself presents it – in terms of the biblical plotline, beginning as Paul does with God and his creation and ending with the coming judgement. Only in this way can we give an effective apologetic for our secular and pagan times, engaging in the marketplace of religious pluralism. Following Paul, as we are faithful to the gospel and defend the faith with respect, clarity and simplicity, challenging the foolishness of unbelieving thought, God will show his mercy and grace. Some will sneer, but others will ask to hear more about this Christ, and still others will turn to Christ in faith and believe unto salvation.

Chapter 6

Earning a Hearing
People-sensitive evangelism

Paul McGee

> We have in England a particular bashfulness in everything that regards religion.
>
> Joseph Addison
> (*The Spectator*, 15 August 1712)

Some things never change!

For many people in the Western world, God is not even on their radar. Church is seen as dull, boring and irrelevant. Christians are seen as narrow-minded party poopers, who simply want to impose their views on others.

The purpose of this chapter is not to show you how to evangelize, but to show you how to engage with people in such a way that they become more receptive to attending an event such as an Alpha course, a carol service or the 'Just 10' series by J.John.

Let's first deal with a stark reality. Is Christianity seen as good news? Are you serious? For many people today such a notion seems more of a joke!

Is it any wonder that within this context, many Christians struggle to share their faith, and many evangelistic meetings are packed full of believers? OK, that's the bad news. But that's not the whole story.

In some areas, the church is growing, faith is communicated relevantly and Christianity really is good news for people. Many of the evangelists that I have come to know through my relationship with J.John are communicating an exciting, relevant message to people without a faith. Venues are crowded. Lives are being transformed.

But what are the factors that help people who currently possess no faith in God to become more receptive to the Christian message? I have identified three. There are countless more, but I think this will provide us with enough insight to get us started.

Cut the cringe

I attended a carol service with my wife Helen some years ago. It had been an event to which I wished I'd been able to bring some friends who would not normally go along to church. Thirty minutes into the service, I felt an overwhelming sense of relief that none of them had been able to make it. I also felt a sense of acute embarrassment and even anger at what I was witnessing.

The speaker seemed to have one goal in mind: 'people must feel condemned by what I have to say'. Personally, I have major issues with such an approach but, that aside, I was wondering how many people listening to him would have even understood his message. At one point he asked, 'Have you been washed in the blood of the Lamb?' In my mind this conjured up images of the local abattoir rather than engaging in a relationship with my Creator. We were also asked, 'Have you repented from your sin and approached the throne of grace?' I wondered whether people who did not normally come to church would feel compelled to come again.

When people cringe they feel uncomfortable. When they feel uncomfortable, their usual response is, 'Get me out of here!' They are not in a place where they are open to listening and exploring ideas.

So did Jesus make people feel uncomfortable? Yes. Those who considered themselves righteous and better than others were indeed uncomfortable listening to his message. But what about other people? The exact opposite is true.

People travelled for miles to hear Jesus speak and to spend time with him. Even young children were not afraid to approach the Rabbi. Jesus caused people to laugh and to think about their lives, their relationships and their society. People felt challenged by what Jesus had to say, but few felt condemned.

So what about today? How do people who currently lack a faith in God feel when they are around you and me? Accepted? Challenged? Or condemned?

I love going out for a pub meal, but I can feel slightly uncomfortable visiting a place I have not been to before. Is it waitress service? Do I go to the bar or will they come to me? Where are the menus? It's a minor thing, but you get the point. People feel uncomfortable around the unfamiliar. The same goes for when we invite people to a Christian event. So let's explore a scenario. I hope the following is not the norm, but I do believe it contains some elements of truth.

You decide to invite someone to your church. Their motives for coming may be mixed, but the good news is, they decide to come. Maybe it's been years since they set foot in a church. On their arrival, they receive a hug from a total stranger, who enthusiastically calls them 'brother' or 'sister'. They sing hymns containing words they do not understand. They look on embarrassed as the worship leader encourages all the adults to join in with the latest kids' worship song and make sure we do all the actions. They sit through a sermon where their knowledge of Greek increases but their day-to-day challenges in life, their doubts and their struggles, remain untouched. At the end of the service, they are asked countless questions by an over-friendly couple who trained with the Gestapo, while drinking weak tea accompanied by a stale biscuit. At the end of the meeting, you ask them if they'd like to come again.

So why are events such as the Alpha course and the 'Just 10' series by J.John so popular and so successful? There are many reasons. But one reason is surely the lack of the cringe factor. Whatever people's background and experience, beliefs and attitudes, they are made to feel comfortable, welcome and accepted.

Maybe next time you are considering a venue for your next evangelistic event, check out your local coffee-house, hotel or pub – and above all, cut the cringe.

Carry on the compassion

I have some slight reservations about the phrase 'friendship evangelism'. I'm sure the intentions are good, but I get the impression that some people's motive is solely to befriend you in order to convert you – and if you are not open to the gospel message, I'll take my friendship elsewhere. Throughout the Gospels, we read that Jesus had compassion (Mark 6:34; 8:2), and in 2 Corinthians 1:3, God is described as 'the Father of compassion'.

But here's the deal: whether people followed Jesus or not, he reached out to them with compassion and loved them. Period.

What about you and me? Will I still reach out and befriend my gay neighbour who has no intention of changing his lifestyle? Will I still spend time listening to my self-obsessed materialistic friend, who thinks people who believe in God are on a par with those who think the moon is made of cheese? What does Jesus say? Love your neighbour. Period.

Over the last few years, Helen and I have got to know and enjoy the company of Cathy and Steve. Steve, by his own admission, does not have a religious bone in his body. I tried to explain that as a Christian, neither do I, but our conversation reached a cul-de-sac and we ended up talking about football instead. Recently Steve found out that his dad is terminally ill with cancer. He asked to come over and see me. We sat down together in my lounge. He cried. Then he cried some more. I sat there. I listened. I didn't talk about God. I felt some of his pain. We drank coffee. We talked about how Steve might make the most of the last few remaining months with his father. We still didn't talk about God. Steve told me I was the only person he could be open and honest with.

I really hope Steve gets to know God. He and Cathy came to a Rob Parsons event on parenting recently. We had a good evening. But Steve might not get to know God. Whatever. I still intend to be his mate. I must carry on the compassion.

Here's another example. I love this story that Tony Campolo tells. He was once working in a different time zone to his own and couldn't sleep. So in the early hours of the morning, he wandered outside to a local dough-nut shop where he found that the local prostitutes con-gregated. While there he overheard a conversation between two of them. A girl named Agnes said to her friend that the next day was her birthday. She talked about how she had never had a birthday party in her life and that tomorrow would be no different.

Tony was moved with compassion. He had an idea. He found out that Agnes came in to the store every night. Tony got the store-owner and his wife involved in organizing a surprise birthday party for Agnes. They arranged for a cake, candles and decorations.

The next night, when Agnes came into the store, they all shouted, 'Surprise!' Agnes was overwhelmed. People began to sing happy birthday and she began to cry. She was so overcome, she could hardly blow out the candles. Rather than cut the cake, she asked if she could take it home instead – just to keep it for a while and savour what had happened.

When Agnes left clutching her cake, Tony led the guests in a prayer for her. The shop-owner turned to Tony and said, 'I didn't realize you were a preacher. What kind of church do you go to?'

Tony replied, 'I belong to a church that throws birthday parties for prostitutes at 3.30 in the morning.'

The shop-owner didn't believe him. 'No you don't. There ain't no church like that. If there was, I'd join it. Yep, I'd join a church like that.'

Tony Campolo doesn't elaborate on what happened after that night. Maybe Agnes is still a prostitute. But at least for that one night, she experienced the love and compassion of God – expressed through people.

I honestly believe that when we see people as people and not as a project to convert, then they begin to see the compassion that drives us. They see our genuineness and they realize we have no hidden agenda. I sense at that point, they may be the ones who want to talk about God.

Curiosity counts

I became a Christian in the early 1980s. My mission in life was to convert the world. All I wanted to do was to tell people about Jesus. My approach was simple: I talk. You listen. Hopefully by the end of my talking, you will pray a prayer and accept Jesus. People rarely did.

Over the years, as I have studied the Gospels, I have become acutely aware that apart from connecting with people through parables, Jesus' main way of engaging people was to ask questions. It seems he was more concerned with dialogue than with giving people a monologue.

I think as Christians, seeking to share our faith, we are often the ones having to answer questions rather than pose them. However, a great way to engage others is to show some curiosity about what they believe. Got a friend who is an atheist? Perhaps rather than launch into the ten reasons why you believe God exists, it might be more appropriate and effective to ask them how they have come to the conclusion that God doesn't exist.

If someone was to ask me, 'How can I believe in a God when there is so much suffering?' I might ask them, 'Well, let's assume there is no God – why do you think there is so much suffering in the world?'

Such questions give us an opportunity to enter into a dialogue and to understand where the other person is coming from. Showing a curiosity in what other people believe shows respect and can also uncover the fact that most people's beliefs are often based on some weak foundations.

Rather than getting into a confrontation with people about whose viewpoint is correct, it's often possible, with the gentle use of questions, to help people to realize the weakness and the shallowness of their argument.

It's important that people don't lose face during this exchange, but that they are encouraged and challenged to explore the big questions of life further.

Helen and I have a friend in Australia called Kelly. She is an atheist. I asked her recently, 'What kind of God don't you believe in?'

She replied, 'An old man with a white beard, sitting on a cloud playing a harp.'

I replied, 'That's good, because I don't believe in a God like that either.'

The more we talked, the more I realized that Kelly was probably not an atheist. Her problem was not to do with the existence of God, but to do with what she perceived as the hypocrisy and double standards of people who claim to be Christians. Questions reveal so much.

Here are four questions that I'd like you to reflect on in relation to some of the people close to you in your world who currently profess no faith:

1. What's going on in their world at the moment? (Divorce, debt, discontentment, children leaving home, promotion, ill parents, etc.?)
2. What's important to them at this time? (Security, peace of mind?)
3. When talking to them, do I listen to understand or listen to defend?
4. Have I communicated my perspective about what I believe?

Jesus rarely preached at people – he engaged with them. He entered into a dialogue. He asked questions. Perhaps our relationships with others will improve, and their receptiveness to what we have to say will increase, when we show a little more concern for their lives and more curiosity about what they believe.

Conclusion

Are people spiritually hungry? Yes, some are. But many are not. Some are completely overwhelmed and side-tracked with the distractions of modern life. Preaching to them will rarely work. Inviting them out of the blue to a church service will rarely meet with a positive response. We have to engage. So remember:

- *Cut the cringe* – create an environment where people feel comfortable being around you.
- *Carry on the compassion* – love people for who they are now. Love with no hidden agenda.
- *Curiosity counts* – show a genuine interest in other people's lives and the beliefs they hold.

Chapter 7

How to People-Fish
1-2-1 evangelism

Anthony Delaney

> We're no longer fishers of men, but keepers of the aquarium, and we spend most of our time swiping fish from each other's bowls.
>
> William Temple, Archbishop of Canterbury (1942–4)[1]

> . . . Jesus went into Galilee, proclaiming the good news of God. 'The time has come,' he said. 'The kingdom of God has come near. Repent and believe the good news!'
>
> **Jesus Calls His First Disciples**
>
> As Jesus walked beside the Sea of Galilee, he saw Simon and his brother Andrew casting a net into the lake, for they were fishermen. 'Come, follow me,' Jesus said, 'and I will send you out to fish for people.' At once they left their nets and followed him. Mark 1:14–18 TNIV

You might expect, from a lot of contemporary evangelism, that when somebody encountered the Jesus of the Gospels, he said, 'Come, follow me and I will make your life easy.'

Lots of evangelistic presentations today seem *me-centred* rather than *Christ-centred* and seem to hinge on this message. I'm not sure what Christians of a bygone age – such as those who feature in *Foxe's Book of Martyrs* (a chronicle published in 1563 of Christians who died for their faith during the Reformation) – would have made of it.

A Martian landing in the UK and looking at the external data of the church today might assume that Jesus had said: 'Come, follow me, and I will make you middle class', 'Come, follow me, and I will make you nice', 'Come, follow me and I will make you build lovely churches', 'Come, follow me and I will make you wear counter-cultural footwear' or 'Come, follow me, and I will make you drink Fairtrade coffee.'

These are the kind of things we might deduce that Jesus had said if we were to examine the standards of much of our Christianity today. He didn't say any of them. But when Jesus called the first of his disciples, he said he was going to make them into something that I think probably totally confused them: *fishers of people*.

This chapter looks at a very important issue, and some pointers and principles on witnessing *one to one* – sometimes called *friendship evangelism* or *personal evangelism*.

How do you become a people-fisher? How do you become better equipped to boldly go and include, invite and involve other people in this spiritual life we're all called into?

As God does not change, Jesus' agenda for you and me today is the same agenda as for those guys he strode up to by the Sea of Galilee two thousand years ago. He is calling us to catch people for his kingdom.

The evangelistic imperative

For us, as for them, that is probably a little bit intimidating. Maybe it will jar with your own background. It may go against the way you were raised. Your personality or culture is such that it would be strange for you to engage in an activity that could be misinterpreted as you trying to impose your worldview on others.

You may say: 'It's not my thing. It might be your thing, and J.John's thing; maybe it's your odd personality type or something, but this is not my thing – it doesn't fit me.'

If you call yourself a believer, a disciple of Jesus, his word to you is the same as the call to those first disciples. So as you read the following verse, I encourage you to do so out loud, putting your name at the beginning, so you can hear the call of Jesus that is coming to *you* in the course of an ordinary day, just as it did to those first disciples. The call doesn't change:

> *X*, come, follow me – and I will make you a fisher of people.

In this one short life there may be all kinds of things I might want Jesus to do for me, or to make me. I might want him to make me better at organizing my time, or to make me a better golfer or a better cook! Regardless of what *I* want him to do for *me*, this is the thing he wants me to do for *him*!

It might not be your thing. It might not be my thing. It patently is *his* thing. He came to seek and save that which is lost. Now Jesus expects us to make his thing, our thing.

Having this desire to go out *people-fishing* is a sign that you have an authentic faith and that the Holy Spirit really is operating in your life.

C. H. Spurgeon (not known for mincing his words) wrote, 'Have you no wish for others to be saved? Then you are not saved yourself. Be sure of that.'

When God came to earth, he came as a man with a message. Jesus was a preacher and a teacher. He was also a highly effective personal evangelist who was fishing for people all the time!

Since the days of Christ, how we do evangelism has evolved considerably. Some people will have the privilege of standing on a platform somewhere and seeing thousands come to Christ at once. They're *fishing with a trawler* and that's fantastic. For most of us, though, the call is to go *people-fishing* with a single rod – one life at a time.

Here are some important principles I try to bear in mind as I do that:

Live as a recipient of good news!

Jesus has a job to do, and he will do it – but the great (and scary) part is, he doesn't want to do it alone. In Mark chapter 1 we read that he 'went into Galilee, proclaiming the good news of God'. We can learn a lot from that summary of his message to help us share our faith one to one.

First of all, do you know that Christianity is *good news*? If you are ever going to be one of those who is ready to share their faith one to one as a joy, not a duty, you have to be convinced that it really is very good news! Every day since Jesus announced that the kingdom of God has arrived, is a day of good news. When you see how good it is, you don't want it to be a private party. It's great to be able to pass out invitations!

I went into the bank and joined the queue with all the other miserable people. But as I queued, instead of being like those around me, I remembered that I'm not. I remembered something of what God had done for me in

Christ. I remembered that I'm loved by God my Father, with an everlasting love. I remembered that he cares for me, called me and adopted me into his family. He forgave my sin, justified me and saved me from hell. I remembered that my life has a purpose. I offered up a silent prayer of gratitude, and as I stood there in the queue, I must have started smiling.

The bored woman behind the counter called me forward and, after taking my request for a new chequebook, asked me in a monotone – like she'd asked everyone else – whether I wanted a review of my account.

I said, 'No thanks, I'm happy.'

She looked at me quizzically (maybe she'd been checking my balance!). 'You're happy?'

I said, 'I am very happy!' (I couldn't hold it in!) 'I am the happiest man you will have in here all day, and it's not dependent on how much I have or don't have. I'm happy because God loves me – and he loves you too!'

I have to admit, I don't do that kind of thing very often! The joy just kind of bubbled up, and now when I go into my bank, this woman always has a smile for me. We've had some more talks since then about the Lord. She's on a journey. It all started when I remembered the gospel is good news, and the kingdom of heaven is not a private party.

You remember what it's like to get good news? When your team won? When you got the news, 'It's a girl!' When your L-plates got ripped up? It's great news. So, you can smile! I'm not talking about some phoney religious grimace. There's a joy in you – God put it there – and it wants to get out!

I remember inviting a guy to come to church with me and he said, 'I'm not going to church – I live opposite one! I see those people every week going in looking miserable and coming out looking gloomy!' Not much of an advert, is it?

We have a lot to smile about in a world in need of joy. The first thing to remember in sharing your faith one to one is that it's *good news*.

Show that people matter

You can go on tours of Israel called 'Following the steps of Jesus', but if you're interested in learning how to share your faith one to one, I'd encourage you to look through the Gospels and follow the *stops* of Jesus.

Think about the times when Jesus, who was very busy and doing something very important, *stopped*. He stopped to fully be with people. He would listen to them. He was interested in them, young and old alike.

This is one of the most important things to remember when you're sharing your faith with an individual. Whoever you are with, give yourself to them as if they are the only person in the world at that moment. Everywhere you go, there are people. Every day, God has been preparing hearts.

One way to show that a person matters is to ask them questions. It is fascinating to observe how many questions Jesus asked in the Gospels. We can try to make ourselves interesting or we can instead focus on the person we're with. You will find people are very interested in anyone who is interested in them! Rebecca Manley Pippert wrote:

> Jesus wants us to see that the neighbour next door or the people sitting next to us on a plane or in a classroom are not interruptions to our schedule. They are there by divine appointment. Jesus wants us to see their needs, their loneliness, their longings, and he wants to give us the courage to reach out to them.[2]

When Jesus was out *people-fishing*, he did it one life at a time and treated each person as a soul that mattered deeply to God.

Call forth a response

The gospel is an invitation with an RSVP on it. Jesus is good news that demands a *response*.

If I told you the taxonomy of the tree outside your house, you might be impressed with my Latin. That's information of a sort. But if I said, 'That tree has got its roots under your house', or 'It's going to fall on your car!', that's information of a different order – it demands that you do something about it!

When people are invited to an event or function most of them respond – it's rude not to! Don't simply share your faith with your non-Christian work colleague or friend, but call forth a response from them. An appropriate way to do this might be to invite them to an evangelistic guest event or Alpha course where they can hear the gospel fully explained.

A recent Tearfund survey said 6 per cent of Britons would be happy to go to church if only they were asked. That's 3 million people who'll sit at home this Sunday waiting for you to bring them a personal invitation.

Call people to repentance

J. I. Packer says:

> Simple assent to the gospel, divorced from a transforming commitment to the living Christ, is by biblical standards less than faith, and less than saving, and to elicit

> only assent of this kind would be to secure only false conversions.[3]

There is a type of evangelism today that sounds more like self-improvement than gospel truth. It says in effect, 'Come to Jesus and he will fill the void inside, making you happy and healthy and wealthy and wise. You only need to repeat these words, and you've got your personal eternal fire insurance.' Jesus said, 'Repent – and believe the good news!'

The emphasis today is to see evangelism purely in terms of process and not crisis. Being born involves a process (pregnancy) but also a crisis (birth). Being born again involves a process but also a crisis. The crisis is when a person responds to the gospel in repentance and faith and becomes a new creature in Christ.

In the Old Testament the word *repent* had the sense of preparing yourself for God to do something. God was saying, 'If you repent of doing the wrong thing I will do something new among you.'

There has to be some ground broken up before a seed of truth will take root. I have found that the most powerful way to encourage people to see the need for repentance is to rehearse with them or remind them of the Ten Commandments. Perhaps this is one of the reasons why J.John's 'Just 10' series has had such remarkable and long-lasting fruit.

Where I live, everyone is a good person! I rarely meet anyone who thinks of themselves as a sinner. Talk about how Jesus saves from sin, and these days many people have no idea what you're talking about. Charles Finney said:

> the Law must prepare the way for the gospel. To overlook this in instructing souls is almost certain to result in

> false hope, the introduction of a false standard of Christian experience, and to fill the Church with false converts. Time will make this plain.[4]

Nowadays, in sharing my faith one to one with people, I ask them if they consider themselves a good person – and I get the inevitable positive answer. I know from my own life that until you see sin as it is, you can't see your need of a Saviour. I was a police officer for many years and before coming to Christ, I would deflect any creeping sense of sin away by pointing to those I'd arrested and reassuring myself that I was not as bad as them!

Then, I encourage people to measure themselves not against Saddam Hussein, Adolf Hitler or Mother Teresa, but against Jesus Christ, who is God's revealed standard of righteousness.

- Ever told a lie? (White ones count.)
- Ever stolen anything? (Expenses, taxes, a library book?)
- Ever murdered? (Jesus equated hatred and anger with murder.)
- Ever looked with lust at or coveted something that wasn't yours?

I then help the person to see that these are Ten *Commandments* (not ten *suggestions*) given by an absolutely holy God. I have found that when I start talking to people (people who moments before were telling me they were good!) about the Ten Commandments and invite them to apply *this* standard to their own lives, they often go very quiet.

People need to know the seriousness of their disease, before they will do what it takes to get the cure. Jesus wanted people to respond *today*, because he knew that otherwise there would be judgement *tomorrow*. Unless people *see* their need to renounce and turn away from sin (true repentance), they won't! They will merely tag Christianity onto their lives, try church for a while as a self-improvement club and, if it doesn't deliver, will fall away and be twice as difficult to reach as before.

There is much talk of friendship evangelism, but a true friend tells you what you need to know even if you might not want to hear it. If I am involved in conversation about spiritual things with people, I tend not to allow myself to be distracted by the many smokescreen questions people throw out. You know the ones: 'What was there before God?', 'How did Noah get all those animals on the ark?' and so on. Usually they're not the real question anyway. These days I ask people whether they know any of the Ten Commandments, and take it from there.

I am confident in this approach because, whether or not they learned the Ten Commandments in Sunday school (increasingly unlikely), the Bible says that God has written them on their hearts. It's not just on tablets of stone – God's law is operating in the conscience he gave them. Since I have done this, I've found that hard cases soften and grown men sometimes even cry. They open up to their need for a Saviour.

Notice, Jesus calls people to repent, *before* he calls them to believe. We call people to believe and hope they'll eventually repent, but it doesn't usually work that way! If people *will* repent, then they will have a new nature, they will hate sin. They will enter the kingdom and trust the King who so freely forgives. It will be a genuine, heartfelt conversion leading to holiness – not the next fad they try on the never-ending pursuit-of-happiness chase.

Capture the urgency!

Tonight before I go to bed, I'm setting my alarm clock for the early hours of the morning, because tonight there is going to be a meteor shower. Ever seen one? I did once, three years ago, and I want to see one again. I'll drag myself out of bed at 3 a.m. and put my dressing-gown on and stand in the back garden and look up, waiting for what occurs as the earth passes through a trail of debris left by a comet. Tiny grains of dust and ice will collide with the earth's atmosphere at speeds of up to 30 miles per second, each creating an arc of incandescent light.

Last time I nearly missed it! When the time came, I lay in bed half asleep, wondering whether I should bother. I thought, 'I have probably missed it anyway, it's cold tonight, and I'm tired.' But I dragged myself up and I went out. I was glad I did. It was the most amazing, breath-taking, unforgettable sight – to see all these meteors coming, flying over the house, from every direction. So many shooting stars! It was like God was putting on the most astonishing firework display, just for me. You understand that I had to *do* something to *experience* it? I had to rearrange my life to see what heaven was up to.

When Jesus came he said that, 'The kingdom of heaven is at hand.' He was saying that his very being ushered in the kingdom in a startling new way. It is near! It is now! It was a message of urgency. If you don't rearrange your life, then you're going to miss out!

God wants us to capture this sense of urgency as we seek to be ambassadors for him to the people we meet, so that the kingdom might be advanced, one life at a time.

Chapter 8

Singing the Song of Salvation
Evangelism through worship

Dave Edwards

> I think worship can be a great evangelistic tool. Someone sitting in a congregation of worshippers hears the word through song, reads it on the screen and sees others responding to God . . . there is something very powerful and moving about being in a group of people who are making that simple, sincere declaration. There is so much about worship that attracts the unchurched unbeliever. Of all the activities of the church, worship is the least selfish and the most pure . . . worship becomes a very powerful testimonial of hope and love to a world living on the edge of despair.
>
> Jim Firth[1]

There has for generations been a great separation in our churches – between worship and evangelism. Evangelism is what we do to get people saved and worship is what they do when they are saved. The received wisdom – often from the seeker movement – is that when we have a guest service we need to dial down the worship, or even abandon it altogether, for fear of making unbelievers sing what they cannot mean, feel uncomfortable and run a mile!

Is this assumption true? Are the two diametrically opposed? My experience – like Jim Firth's – is that this is far from the case.

A young man walked into one of our meetings. A friend had invited him and I knew that he had only just come out of prison. He looked fairly 'streetwise' and unchurchy. Although we were doing all that we could to make people feel 'at home', I was a little concerned as to just how unhelpful the time of sung worship was going to be for our visitor. We led about fifteen minutes of worship, some of which felt fairly intimate. I was grateful for what the Lord was doing, yet still a little anxious for our guest. It was only as I sat down that I could see that there were tears rolling down his cheeks. He later told me how this time of worship had been particularly significant for him. It was only one of the ways in which God was drawing this young man to himself, but it was important nonetheless.

We sing songs of worship to give glory to God and yet it seems that throughout the years he has graciously chosen to use these songs to communicate to others the realities of his nature and love.

It is interesting to consider that the church's first big evangelistic meeting was birthed out of a time of Spirit-filled praise. This time of worship caused people to be puzzled and to ask questions: 'What does this mean?' (Acts 2:12 NIV). The stage was then set for Peter to stand up and communicate the gospel, proclaiming the death and resurrection of Jesus Christ. Later on, in Acts 16, we see Paul's and Silas' time of sung worship in prison in Philippi leading to a powerful move of the Spirit and the conversion of the jailer and his family.

We know that sung worship is powerful but we are also concerned not to put any unnecessary barriers in the way of people who are enquiring about the Christian faith. If a meeting is put on to help those who don't yet believe in Jesus, should we really expect them to sing 'our songs'? We have seen people looking uncomfortable during what seem more like Christian 'knees-ups' and many of us can remember feelings of alienation ourselves from our early days as Christians or enquirers.

What role should sung worship have in evangelism? Can we invite people to experience the wonder and joy of worshipping God while still being sensitive to the questions and issues that this may raise for many?

I have a conviction about how wonderfully God can use music and song because of my own story. I grew up in a family that didn't go to church and I was happy to keep my distance from Christians whom I felt had become a bit 'over keen' on God. I believed that there probably was a loving Creator God and I knew about Jesus from school, but I didn't want to get too involved!

When I left home in Kent to go and be a student in Nottingham, the last thing that I had on my mind to do was to go to church. I was excited about music, sport and the possibility of new relationships; I couldn't wait to be a student. To my surprise, I found myself feeling lonely and depressed as I acclimatized to a new life away from everything that was familiar to me. To my added surprise, I found myself at the local parish church one Sunday morning – responding to the invitation of the university chaplain. It was a Harvest service and I was made to feel very welcome. I can't remember much about the content of the service but I can remember that as I joined in with the songs, it felt like a 'home-coming'. As they sang old Harvest hymns, I could sense the love of the God who had graciously watched over me all of my life. As they sang more modern choruses, I realized that I was among a people who were enjoying God's nearness and care. There was something truly good, beautiful and real here.

Many things helped me during those early days of coming to faith in Christ, but I am sure that the experience of God's presence in worship was highly significant for me. I had long had a passion for the power of music and loved the way that a great song could somehow speak the language of the soul, but now there was an even richer dimension. As I listened to and sang these Christian songs and hymns, I could see how God's truth could be carried on the wings of beautiful melodies and enter into our hearts. I was also discovering how there was a special sense in which we could enjoy God's presence in times of worship. Worship songs had been evangelistic to me: they spoke the gospel of Christ into my heart and they awakened me to the possibility of an intimate relationship with him.

As I watched people lead worship and as I listened to recordings of Christian artists, the desire to have an equally rich walk with God grew within me. Ever since those days I have sensed a two-fold desire in my heart as I lead people in corporate worship. I want people to *hear* the gospel of the Lord Jesus Christ and also to *experience* something of his loving, glorious presence. I have had the privilege of leading worship at many area-wide evangelistic meetings and also the honour of singing to small groups in schools, homes or nursing homes. Wherever it is, it seems that songs can be a real gift both to communicate the good news and to provide space for the Holy Spirit to minister to people's hearts.

So the divorce was unnecessary! Worship and evangelism *can* belong together – but in what ways exactly does this work out in practice? Here are six things worship can do that connect evangelistically. Dynamic, New Testament worship . . .

. . . can declare the Gospel

The story of Jesus' life, death and resurrection is God's power among us to transform lives (Rom. 1:16).

When we lead worship at evangelistic events, we try to include songs and hymns which tell of all that Jesus has done for us. It is not always true, but for many enquirers it will be easier to sing more 'descriptive' songs than intimate worship songs; we need to think about what we are asking people to sing. We would normally use a couple of more celebratory/praise/ gospel songs or hymns before using a well-chosen, slightly more personal song. Rules are probably made to be broken in this field but the principle can be helpful.

The gospel proclaimed in song seems to prepare the way for the preaching of the gospel later on. We have found that appropriate, well-presented solos can be very powerful here alongside congregational singing.

. . . can clear the spiritual air

It seems that sung worship is a tool that the Lord often chooses to use to usher his presence and his kingdom in. In 2 Chronicles 20 Jehoshaphat 'appointed men to sing to the LORD and to praise him for the splendour of his holiness as they went out at the head of the army' (2 Chr. 20:21 NIV). The battle against Israel's enemies was won simply as they sang, 'Give thanks to the LORD, for his love endures for ever.'

In Psalm 8 we read that 'From the lips of children and infants you have ordained praise because of your enemies, to silence the foe and the avenger' (Ps. 8:2 NIV). Our battle is not against flesh and blood, but God has chosen to push back spiritual darkness through the power of simple praise. It is not surprising that so many evangelists choose to have sung worship before they preach. They sense a better spiritual atmosphere and a greater openness.

. . . can be a communal testimony

Hearing someone tell their story of how God has worked in their life can be very powerful. When we sing together as believers there is a kind of 'communal testimony' as we testify to our experience of God's goodness and faithfulness. This can be quite compelling.

I remember, soon after becoming a Christian myself, going with my brother Simon to an evangelistic event. Simon had been quite a vocal atheist/agnostic up to this stage and I was a little nervous about what he would make of this event. As we came into the back of the meeting, the worship had already started. Simon describes what he found:

> I was expecting the meeting to be dull and the church virtually empty. I was surprised to find the church full, both of people and of passionate song. Something struck me as being very real about the singing. I sensed that there was life and joy and freedom amongst these people and it had a profound impact on me.

Simon believes that this experience of 'true worship' was the beginning of his opening up to the gospel and to Christ. He is still a committed Christian to this day.

In the world there is often so much despair. It is a wonderful thing to see a people who are united in their hope and able to celebrate together despite their difficulties and pain.

. . . can speak to the heart

All music is a God-given gift and a universal language – the language of the heart. Some people who are not moved by stirring oratory are moved to tears by music – this is because it bypasses the mind and touches the heart.

God reveals his beauty through the majesty of creation, and music is a part of this. This should encourage us to choose good melodies and to play skilfully. Having said this, the Lord often uses simple things to display his power. He can anoint the melody of a shepherd boy's harp to silence a demon (1 Sam. 16:14–23) or a trumpet blast and a shout to bring down city walls (Josh. 6:20). We want to play as well as we can while earnestly seeking him for his glorious touch.

. . . can move people from spectating to participating

Though we don't want to *force* people to sing, it is great to give folk a way of being active rather than passive in a meeting. Joining in with a song may be a significant first step of faith for someone. During the sung worship we are seeking to give of our praise, our hearts and our lives in response to the goodness of God. This is a natural preparation for any invitation to respond to the gospel that may be given as part of the preaching later on.

. . . can be a place of divine encounter

We know that God is everywhere, but as Graham Kendrick has said, 'He can also choose to be somewhere.'

We can meet with God through any of the arts, through fellowship or through silence, yet it seems that he has particularly ordained that we can draw near to him through praise and worship (Pss 95:1–2; 100:4). The songs are a vehicle for us to fix our eyes on the Lord and to turn our hearts back to him. As we draw near to God, he draws near to us (Jas 4:8).

We want people to hear the truth but we also long for them to experience the presence of God himself. In this often hectic world we can serve people by providing holy space to allow them to meet with God. Our prayer is that a longing will be stirred in them for something, or should we say Someone, that they were made for.

A friend of mine called Maggie went into a church as someone who was searching after God. She comments:

> Though the music was simple I could sense the passion, conviction and unity of people as they sang.
>
> The worship was both beautiful and challenging. The intimacy of the songs and of God's presence was calling me to respond in a deep way. I felt humbly aware of my sin and at the same time wonderfully aware of God's overwhelming love.

For Maggie this was the beginning of a new walk with God that continues now, twenty-six years later.

Of course, we shouldn't restrict evangelistic worship to our church or evangelistic meetings. There is something very versatile about music, and a good musician, band or choir can take their music to all sorts of venues, clubs, schools and institutions. It is good to pray for opportunities to take the song of God's love out into our communities. Sometimes we may feel led to present a mixed repertoire, adding in some well-known pop songs for people to listen to or maybe sing along to.

Some great opportunities have developed in local schools and nursing homes and in a local brain injury unit.

It is important that we go to serve and build relationships. We are not going just to drop a 'worship bomb' on people, but we are seeking to offer something that will be helpful and encouraging to folk, meeting them where they are.

Leading worship evangelistically – three suggestions

1. Be sensitive

It is worth considering how hard it can be for folk to come along to some of our meetings. For many of us, it is helpful to recall the time in our lives when we first came along to Christian events. I remember being really nervous about being controlled, manipulated or even brainwashed. I was quite unsure as to what these Christians did at their meetings!

We need to do all that we can to put people at ease. Jesus talked about being like a shepherd who leaves the ninety-nine safe sheep to go after the one that is lost. We need to consider how we communicate – the language we use and the songs we choose.

The truth is that it is very difficult to compile a worship song set of totally 'seeker-sensitive' congregational songs. I used to be very strict about using appropriate lyrics in songs, but if you get too narrow you can suck the life out of the worship. I'm not sure that Spirit-filled worship can ever totally fit into a 'seeker-sensitive' model, but the ways in which we welcome people, explain what we are doing and introduce songs can make a real difference. I still think it is worth looking through the lyrics of the songs that we are singing and praying for wisdom to choose the songs that the Holy Spirit wants to use in a particular meeting.

Often, it is how we frame the songs that really matters. Having welcomed people, I sometimes say something like, 'We are now going to sing three songs that celebrate God's goodness. Feel free to join in if you would like to, or just to listen to the words if you prefer. We will begin by standing, but if you want to sit after a while, feel free.' I used to give people the choice of standing or sitting from the outset, but this can create an unhelpful divide right at the start. All standing together is clear and simple and is less likely to make anyone feel 'exposed' or unsure.

2. *Be real*

In my experience, people are very wary of hype and pretence – they long to see something that is genuine.

Paul wrote to the Galatians to assure them that they didn't need any religious 'extras' to be pleasing to God. It was simply through faith in Jesus that they were pleasing to him (Gal. 3:1–3,26; 5:1). We need to pray that we can shake off any 'churchy' culture or language that might be a barrier to people simply coming to Christ. Humour can be very helpful here to keep things light and to show that we don't take ourselves too seriously!

Alongside the strong praise songs, we often include a song that comes more from a place of brokenness and longing. We could introduce the song by explaining that it was written by someone who experienced God's faithfulness and love during a time of suffering or pain. Often people are far more able to connect with our faith at this level than with something more 'triumphalistic'.

We are giving them permission to draw near to God, bringing their pain and their doubts. Leading worship evangelistically is a ministry of grace.

3. Be prayerful

It is important that we don't seek to rely on great songs or a fabulous band. We need to pray that we will be led by the Holy Spirit and that he will make his presence wonderfully known in the meeting.

Of course, it is worth remembering that evangelism is not 'one size fits all'. Some folk may really not be in the place yet to appreciate being part of a time of sung worship. We need to cooperate with the Lord and try to perceive what he is doing in people's lives.

Conclusion: the heart of the matter is the matter of the heart

As I reflect back on my own conversion and as I listen to others, I am aware that although the songs were helpful, it was the love of Christ among his people that really impacted me. Good music is the 'icing on the cake' of a loving, welcoming Christian community. Obviously, we should play as skilfully as we can, but people will put up with some very simple worship if they can sense God's love at work among us.

Perhaps the most powerful evangelistic worship is not our public praise but the hidden times alone or in small groups when we are transformed by encountering God's heart and beauty. A community that is entering into 'true' worship will find themselves caught up with God's glory and his passion to reach out to every man, woman and child. Isaiah offered himself for God's mission after he had encountered God's beauty and holiness in worship (Isa. 6). Paul and Barnabas were set apart for evangelistic mission following a time of extended worship and prayer (Acts 13:1–4).

Our greatest need is to draw near to God and experience his love. A people who are enjoying God in worship should be a people who are caught up with Calvary love and are compelled to share this love with others. The love of Christ compels us (2 Cor. 5:14).

Evangelistic worship is all about knowing God's heart and being a channel for him to draw people close to himself. He longs to welcome people home; his heart is full of compassion.

> While he was still a long way off, his father saw him and was filled with compassion for him; he ran to his son, threw his arms around him and kissed him.
>
> Luke 15:20 NIV

> May the peoples praise you, O God; may all the peoples praise you.
>
> Psalm 67:3 NIV

May our worship of almighty God be an encounter with his Spirit as we declare his truth. May we worship in such a way that unbelievers discern his presence in our midst and begin a journey which ends in them coming to sing a song of salvation for themselves as they receive his divine embrace.

Chapter 9

The Best Boat to Fish From
Evangelism through the local church

David McDougall

> I am convinced that there is no evangelistic force so powerful as a loving, outward-looking local church. It is the key to evangelism in this age that is suspicious of the high-powered sales technique, and at the same time well aware of the emptiness of materialism, the breakdown of relationships, and the shortness of life.
>
> Michael Green[1]

Some have suggested that the role of an ordained minister is no job for an evangelist! As an evangelist who is also an ordained minister of the Church of England, I have discovered that the local church affords a unique opportunity to reach many people of all ages and backgrounds. Colossians 4:5–6 is a life verse for me:

> make the most of every opportunity. Let your conversation be always full of grace, seasoned with salt, so that you may know how to answer everyone (NIV).

I attempt to make the most of every opportunity that comes my way as a church-planting vicar.

This chapter is not just for those in church leadership but for all of us as Christians to explore the amazing untapped potential there is for doing evangelism through a local church congregation. Every day there are endless opportunities – I wish I could utilize them all!

At my induction service here I was given the charge of the 'Cure of Souls' in the parish (as every Anglican vicar is) – an awesome responsibility but also an immense opportunity. I want to offer six principles for effective local church evangelism.

1. Be incarnational

God becoming man shows us that authentic mission is *relational*. Jesus was people-centred and loved being where people were. He attracted crowds but there are endless examples of him visiting homes, businesses and small groups. We need to imitate him in our mission.

Too often evangelism is seen as a disembodied, hit-and-run affair rather than a relational, long-term exercise – a process.

Jesus found Zacchaeus in the tree, increased the wine at a wedding and made breakfast for a few men. He prayed for the sick and he listened to the cynic. He walked with people and listened to their questions. He cried over Jerusalem and felt great sadness over the death of a friend. Jesus was involved in the humdrum process of everyday human life.

God longs for his kingdom to *break in* and *break out* in the daily encounters we have. God is longing for us to have restored confidence that wherever we go, we take his kingdom with us. We are channels of his love, peace, grace, purpose and power.

2. Look to respond to felt needs

The church I lead in London – St Saviour's, Sunbury – was a plant from a larger Anglican church (St Stephen's, Twickenham). When the team that was going to plant the church first got going, we *prayer walked* the local streets and put a glossy postcard through every door, welcoming people to our meetings and letting them know what was going on at their local church.

Around this time a city-wide mission to London, 'Soul in the City', was taking place. We dovetailed our activities with this and organized some clean-up campaigns to tidy up the local area, and a gig with a band called The Tribe.

All this caused a real stir in the community and people began to talk about the church in a positive way! Trust in the local church began to be built again. Since then we have essentially been finding ways to serve our community in order to reach it with the love of God. To do this we have asked ourselves, *What are the felt needs in our community?* How can we serve people in a way that genuinely meets local need?

We began to reorder the church building and make it into a flexible space. By simply removing pews and making a few minor alterations, we ended up with a large and versatile space that could be used every day and not just for worship for a few hours on a Sunday. Straight away we began a pre-school drop-in and an older people's club.

Our pre-school drop-in ('Kiddiwinks') is unashamedly run by Christians. The group meets on two midweek mornings and often has more than 120 people present, all building friendships with each other, happy to be in the church building and creating firm contacts with Christians in our church. It is not a Mums and

Toddlers group that has rented our building and has little to do with the church. It is very Christ-centred and Christian-led.

Through this ministry we have come into contact with all kinds of real needs within the community: poverty, parenting issues and the need for counselling are but a few. It is from this group that scores of children have come through for Dedication or Baptism. It is such a fantastic service and outreach to the local community.

The demand for this group has been such that we have had to start a third drop-in group for pre-school children ('Noah's Ark'). This group is a mini midweek service with play, songs, Bible stories and prayer. It has taken off and now has a regular thirty attending it!

Our older people's drop-in ('Coffee and Chat') is a two-hour midweek café. This group has risen to over forty. They have galvanized into their own community and regularly visit the local pub and have garden parties, quiz nights and theatre trips. It gives me great satisfaction that the local church has facilitated this, and many of these folk are now regular at church and some have attended the Alpha course.

We have been running parenting courses, family fun days and a children's holiday club, and we are starting something called 'Who Let the Dads Out' – a Saturday morning drop-in so that young mums can get a break. There are endless opportunities through the local church as it seeks to reach out and help people on *their* terms, not *ours*.

3. Be there in moments that matter

The occasional offices of Baptisms, weddings and funerals (or 'hatch, match and dispatch', as they are known by vicars!) provide a very natural point of contact with unbelievers at vulnerable and life-changing times in their lives, when they are often more open to the spiritual dimension of life. These are especially relevant for the Church of England, which as the established church is the church of the vast majority of unchurched people.

Dedications and Baptisms

When a new baby is born, the parents often experience an instinctive and inexplicable desire to thank *someone* for that child. Some parents work out that this is God and others are open to the suggestion! We need to honour that desire to express gratitude and find ways that are helpful and appropriate for them to express it. To do so will assist them in their spiritual journey towards God himself.

Lots of unchurched people come to me requesting to have their baby 'done'! There are some churches that will not baptize infants of unbelievers and so miss out on this opportunity for mission. If Baptism is not appropriate, I would strongly suggest offering a service of Dedication instead.

I hold an open office on a Monday evening so that parents can come and talk it through with me as to what they want. They usually come wanting Baptism because they are not aware of our Dedication option. After an initial conversation, many people don't really want the serious commitment that Baptism requires but *do* want to express thanks to God, name their child and ask God to bless their child. These Dedication services are at our main morning service; they have Godparents; there is a Certificate; every child is given a book of Bible stories and a Bible verse is chosen especially for them; relatives and friends come en masse; and there is a tremendous sense of occasion.

My training vicar, Revd Ian Pusey, introduced me to such a policy and in his parish they had so many families wanting Dedication that it had to be moved to Sunday afternoons. Many people choose this service. It allows the children to decide for themselves whether to be baptized when they are older, as this really is a sign of personal belief and trust in Jesus Christ.

Dedicating children means that for unchurched people who do not (yet) believe, we are not asking them to say promises that cause them a lack of integrity by stating what they do not believe. Many parents have been put off church because, when they were younger, religion was pushed on them too heavily and they are still in reaction against that now.

Many visitors have come to these initiation services. Our church is always packed on those Sundays! It's exciting and dynamic, providing an amazing opportunity for a presentation of the gospel, and we rarely miss it! We have found that Christians telling their personal story of faith at these services is incredibly powerful. Once last year, a mum described how God had blessed her with her adopted child – the story melted all of us and people still talk about it. It drew people to faith. Story is so powerful and we need to use it more in our meetings.

For Christians who are regularly attending church, we offer Baptism either by *sprinkling* (for infants) or, more commonly now, by *full immersion* (for children and above). Baptism services include personal stories from the candidates, if they are old enough, and the talk given tends to be evangelistic in nature. Often people decide to be baptized because they attended a Baptism service! The symbolism of it and the witness of it are so powerful, that people are deeply affected by these services.

Weddings

One family wedding I attended as a guest really left me very annoyed. The vicar didn't welcome people at the start or say goodbye. It was performed dutifully with no warmth, charm or relevance to the couple. He literally opened the prayer book and read the service, closed it and left the church. I ran after him! I could not help myself, and challenged him on what he had just done.

Many of our relatives do not know Jesus and this unhelpful minister was not helping us reach them with eternal hope – in fact it was counter-productive and he was putting them off even seeking God! It was such a squandered open door! Weddings are an amazing opportunity to communicate the gospel. The whole process – the preparation, rehearsal and order of the wedding service – is bursting with opportunity for God to be at work.

Welcoming, settling people into church (a strange environment for many people these days) and then communicating relevantly is essential. Allowing the service to reflect the personalities of the couple is attainable through the choice of music, readings, poems and prayers, and by involving their friends and relatives where possible.

The talk at a wedding service is an amazing opportunity. It is my personal practice to write a fresh talk for every wedding (and every funeral) so that I make sure that it's 'fresh manna' and that there is no danger of the message being 'stale' or 'mouldy'.

Using humour is helpful, and so is offering some tools for making a marriage work. Couples really listen and so do the congregation, especially if you have your talk in note form so that you can make good eye contact with all those you are speaking to. In front of us at every wedding is a host of different and complicated marital situations. It is a great opportunity to speak into some of the hurt, frustrations and pain in these marriages.

We should never underestimate the power of these occasional offices to connect people to Christ. Once, when returning to my church office, which was a room off the main service area, I could hear a man crying. I walked nearer to my office and realized that there was a man on the floor weeping. I asked him if he was OK. He said that he had been so overcome by the service that he was just getting his life sorted out with God, and did I mind him being there for a little while? I will never forget that experience.

There have been some wonderful evangelistic moments in many weddings over the years. I remember in one parish a whole family came to Christ through one wedding service. Over twenty years, I have conducted literally hundreds of weddings and have had the privilege of speaking about God to many thousands of people who never normally come near a church.

Funerals

Someone has commented that 'every funeral is our own', meaning that when a person attends the funeral of another, they are brought face to face with their *own* mortality. Perhaps this is why I find that people listen at funerals and there is a window of opportunity into a person's soul that is closed in the normal course of life.

When someone dies in our community, it is always a delicate and important time. We are keen to help the grieving families to create a funeral service that honours their loved one and is helpful to those present at the service. Services of Thanksgiving are a powerful and effective outreach to literally hundreds of people every week.

We have seen the most amazing opportunities in the pre-funeral visit, in the service itself and at the wake afterwards. Pre-funeral visits are essential. It is when we listen and learn about our community. It is when we can make notes on the deceased person so that the service is personal and special for the family. I listen out for funny stories as well as the important contribution that the person has made to their lives. Humour is so helpful in lifting the atmosphere and bringing joy into a difficult time of life. A funeral service should reflect the person who has died; if it doesn't, then the service could have been for anyone. I always offer to pray at the end of a house visit and am rarely turned down. One house visit last year ended in the whole family and I kneeling hand in hand on the floor in prayer. It was a moment I will never forget – the presence of God was so strong in that house.

One service recently included the laying on of hands for those needing the comfort of God. This was extraordinary, but the situation demanded it. There was an unusual amount of outward emotion and so my curate, who was leading the prayers, gently laid hands on those who were finding it impossible to cope. It brought peace and strength to those grieving, and that service will be remembered for a long time.

On another occasion, at a wake, my curate, Andy Sachs, and I had a queue of people wanting to buy us pints and talk to us about Jesus. On this occasion two spiritualists caught us up in conversation and one of them was very interested in doing Alpha.

At yet another recent funeral, I had a long conversation with a brother and sister who had just lost their dad. They were in their early twenties and because of the loss they were rethinking what direction their lives were taking. We had a wonderful talk together and they asked me for all kinds of advice.

The talk at the funeral service is an important opportunity to communicate something of the gospel. Over the years I have learnt to look for a bridge between something of the deceased's character and an aspect of God. For example, I recently took a man's funeral and I was told that he was a very 'selfless' person. Perfect! I talked about the selflessness of Christ. On another occasion I was told that the lady who had died had been a 'great listener', and so I talked about our God, who is interested in every detail of our lives and will listen to us 24/7. Finding the 'bridge' is a great way of making sure we are being personal about the deceased and then bringing in the Christian message.

Funerals, handled well, are talked about a great deal in any community and we have seen some wonderful fruit through this vital pastoral ministry. Both ministers and church members need to wake up to this important opportunity for outreach.

4. Use the liturgical calendar

Christmas and Easter – not a year goes by without them! They are two festivals on the church's liturgical calendar that are deeply embedded in the national psyche.

Some Christians are like Oliver Cromwell, who banned Christmas in 1647. They are quick to point out that it's *folk religion* with pagan origins and are very wary of it. I take the view that we need to *redeem Christmas for Christ* and use this opportunity fully for the gospel. Free publicity of the season is in every department store and dominates radio and TV as the day approaches. What a superb opportunity!

'We joined your church because of the magical nature of the Christmas Midnight Communion service,' one couple told me. Amazing, isn't it, that people want to come to church at midnight! So *when* they come, it is essential that a clear presentation of the Christian message is given. Something relevant. Something fun. Something they will remember. I always try to use the shop slogans for Christmas. One local shop's slogan was 'A Gift for Giving'. I thought it was a perfect title for a Christmas message – after all, 'forgiving' is just what Jesus came to do!

Carol services can be creative and imaginative. They do not need to be complicated because simplicity is usually more powerful. We live in a visual age, so colour and images are important. Publicity needs to be really good – it's worth doing professionally rather than on a photocopier that is running out of ink. The members of the church need to be *intentionally invitational* about telling their friends – a carol service is the easiest one in the year to invite people to. They nearly always say yes! Have lots of free booklets by J.John or someone else whom you think writes relevantly about the season.

Easter is still very under-used by the church as a time of outreach, and yet the cross is the crux of the message. One year we had an Easter Prayer Labyrinth, which we ran for a week. Local schools picked it up and many people journeyed through it, thinking about and experiencing different aspects of the last days of Jesus here on earth. It was a great way of reaching out to all kinds of people in our community.

5. Serve your immediate community

The institutions in the parish – hospitals, prisons and schools – are often in great need of assistance concerning religious provision. This is especially true of schools, which mostly do not have their own chaplains, are required to do religious assemblies by law and are sometimes ill equipped to do so.

The schools in our area are very welcoming and we have more openings than we can possibly handle. We are seeking to reach as many children with the Christian message as possible. Assemblies, RE lessons, carol services, Christian unions, church visits and having church members as school governors are all ways we have been able to be fruitfully involved in the local schools.

Two local secondary schools are running Youth Alpha courses. Bishop Wand Church of England secondary school allowed us to run a week of mission as part of Hope 08, which included debates, RE lessons, assemblies, anger management sessions, detached work in the playgrounds and a rock concert on a Friday night.

6. Invite people on a journey

The Alpha course, subtitled 'an opportunity to explore the meaning of life', is an introductory course that explains the basics of Christianity. Pioneered by Nicky Gumbel of Holy Trinity, Brompton, the course runs in churches, as well as prisons and universities, the world over. Over 2 million people in the UK and 11 million worldwide have now attended an Alpha course. The course has been run by tens of thousands of churches of all denominations across the world.

We have run many Alpha courses and have seen lots of people become Christians through it. The genius of Alpha is that it is not a one-off event but an expression of process evangelism in which people are invited to embark on a journey of faith exploration. For us, people often do Alpha when they have been known to us for quite a while, often having made contact with us in one of the ways mentioned above. I do not need to explain further about Alpha here, because information about it is available from many other sources, especially the main Alpha website at uk.alpha.org. I cannot recommend Alpha enough; it has been the beginning of faith for so many people and God is really blessing it. When participants come back after the whole course and share with the church at Sunday meetings, it is always so exciting, encouraging and faith-building.

Every aspect of pastoral ministry contains an opportunity to connect people to Christ. It's so exciting, and as an evangelist who is also a church leader, I am continuously surrounded by openings. In this chapter I have only scratched the surface of how we can reach out through the local church. I hope this discussion has inspired you to make the most of each opportunity!

Chapter 10

Demonstrating the Good News
Social action and evangelism

Greg Downes

> Our way of sharing the Good News may not be only by preaching. Both personal evangelism and personal service are expressions of compassion. Both are forms of witness to Jesus Christ.
>
> John Stott[1]

In 2008, a worldwide commission of evangelical theologians declared that Christians must not separate social action and evangelism.

Dr Justin Thacker, Head of Theology at the Evangelical Alliance, presented the biblical, historical and ethical imperative for a holistic understanding of the gospel to the World Evangelical Alliance Theological Commission in Bangkok, Thailand. The commission concluded that if evangelical Christians are to be true to their identity as evangelicals, and true to the good news of Jesus Christ as they understand it, then these two aspects of their ministry and service cannot and must not be separated.

Some readers may well be asking why it took an international commission of theologians to conclude in 2008 what the Bible declared 2,000 years ago.

> You are the salt of the earth. But if the salt loses its saltiness, how can it be made salty again? It is no longer good for anything, except to be thrown out and trampled by men.
>
> You are the light of the world. A city on a hill cannot be hidden. Neither do people light a lamp and put it under a bowl. Instead they put it on its stand, and it gives light to everyone in the house. In the same way, let your light shine before men, that they may see your good deeds and praise your Father in heaven.
>
> Matthew 5:13–16 NIV

Let's consider three things from this statement of Jesus as we reflect on the role of social action and evangelism.

You *are* the good news

The medium *is* the message. We are not just called to *preach* good news but to *be* good news. Jesus told his disciples, 'you are the light of the world'. I'm glad that's in black and white, because if a preacher said that to his congregation today, we would assume he was being heretical. *You* are Jesus' twenty-first-century disciple. *You* are the light of the world! *You* may well be the only gospel that somebody ever reads.

I am a big fan of West End musicals. I recently went to see *Les Miserables* for the umpteenth time. Invariably it has me in tears because it is such a powerful story of redemption. *Les Miserables* ('The Wretched') was originally a novel written by Victor Hugo (1802–85) in 1862. It is a moving and profound story set near Paris prior to the French Revolution of 1789. It was this novel that was made into a blockbuster musical in 1980 by Claude-Michel Schönberg (music) and Alain Boublil (lyrics).

Jean Valjean, the main character in the story, has just been released from nineteen years in prison for stealing a loaf of bread to keep his sister's family from starvation. Upon release he is given hospitality by the godly Bishop of Digne, Myriel, but, hardened by his incarceration, Valjean steals and makes off with the Bishop's silver. He is apprehended by the law and brought back to the Bishop's residence. I will allow Hugo's classic narrative to speak for itself:

> The door opened. A singular and violent group made its appearance on the threshold. Three men were holding a fourth man by the collar. The three men were gendarmes; the other was Jean Valjean. A brigadier of gendarmes, who seemed to be in command of the group, was standing near the door. He entered and advanced to the Bishop, making a military salute.
>
> 'Monseigneur—' said he.
>
> At this word, Jean Valjean, who was dejected and seemed overwhelmed, raised his head with an air of stupefaction.
>
> 'Monseigneur!' he murmured. 'So he is not the curé?'
>
> 'Silence!' said the gendarme. 'He is Monseigneur the Bishop.'
>
> In the meantime, Monseigneur Bienvenu had advanced as quickly as his great age permitted.
>
> 'Ah! Here you are!' he exclaimed, looking at Jean Valjean. 'I am glad to see you. Well, but how is this? I gave you the candlesticks too, which are of silver like the rest, and for which you can certainly get two hundred francs. Why did you not carry them away with your forks and spoons?'
>
> Jean Valjean opened his eyes wide, and stared at the venerable Bishop with an expression which no human tongue can render any account of.

'Monseigneur,' said the brigadier of gendarmes, 'so what this man said is true, then? We came across him. He was walking like a man who is running away. We stopped him to look into the matter. He had this silver –'

'And he told you,' interposed the Bishop with a smile, 'that it had been given to him by a kind old fellow of a priest with whom he had passed the night? I see how the matter stands. And you have brought him back here? It is a mistake.'

'In that case,' replied the brigadier, 'we can let him go?'

'Certainly,' replied the Bishop.

The gendarmes released Jean Valjean, who recoiled.

'Is it true that I am to be released?' he said, in an almost inarticulate voice, and as though he were talking in his sleep.

'Yes, thou art released; dost thou not understand?' said one of the gendarmes.

'My friend,' resumed the Bishop, 'before you go, here are your candlesticks. Take them.'

He stepped to the chimney-piece, took the two silver candlesticks, and brought them to Jean Valjean. The two women looked on without uttering a word, without a gesture, without a look which could disconcert the Bishop.

Jean Valjean was trembling in every limb. He took the two candlesticks mechanically, and with a bewildered air.

'Now,' said the Bishop, 'go in peace. By the way, when you return, my friend, it is not necessary to pass through the garden. You can always enter and depart through the street door. It is never fastened with anything but a latch, either by day or by night.'

Then, turning to the gendarmes:

'You may retire, gentlemen.'

> The gendarmes retired.
>
> Jean Valjean was like a man on the point of fainting.
>
> The Bishop drew near to him, and said in a low voice:
>
> 'Do not forget, never forget, that you have promised to use this money in becoming an honest man.'
>
> Jean Valjean, who had no recollection of ever having promised anything, remained speechless. The Bishop had emphasised the words when he uttered them. He resumed with solemnity:
>
> 'Jean Valjean, my brother, you no longer belong to evil, but to good. It is your soul that I buy from you; I withdraw it from black thoughts and the spirit of perdition, and I give it to God.'[2]

Jean Valjean's life is never the same. He has an encounter with lavish grace. He cannot believe his ears as he realizes that he is *not* to be charged: 'Is it true that I am to be released?' he states incredulously. He later turns to God and seeks to live his life with integrity and humility.

Bishop Myriel *demonstrated* the good news of grace, forgiveness and restoration – and it was this living epistle that got through to Jean Valjean and changed his life forever.

William Wilberforce (1759–1833), MP for Hull and later Bramber, was a tireless campaigner for the abolition of slavery. He was a man who knew that Christianity was meant to be lived out in practical ways:

> Is it not the great end of religion, and, in particular, the glory of Christianity, to extinguish the malignant passions; to curb the violence, to control the appetites, and to smooth the asperities of man; to make us compassionate and kind, and forgiving one to another; to make us good husbands, good fathers, good friends; and to

> render us active and useful in the discharge of the relative social and civil duties?[3]

Recognizing the social evil of slavery in his own day, he made an unshakable resolve:

> so enormous, so dreadful, so irremediable did the Trade's wickedness appear that my own mind was completely made up for Abolition. Let the consequences be what they would, I from this time determined that I would never rest until I had effected its abolition.[4]

The selling of slaves was made illegal in 1807 but it wasn't until 28 August 1833 – a month after Willberforce's death – that the Slavery Abolition Act fully ended slavery, with slaves in the British Empire being emancipated. This was largely the victory of one man who was truly a bright light in the world in which he lived. Will we follow his example?

Faith works

One of the great rediscoveries of the Reformation was the biblical truth of *justification by faith*. The German reformer Martin Luther (1483–1546) waged a war against the spiritual abuses of his day, which included the erroneous view that an individual's right standing with God could be obtained by good deeds.

Sadly, as so often is the case, some of us who are children of the Reformation have thrown the baby out with the bathwater and have a very ambivalent view of good works in any context. The regrettable legacy of the desire to defend this great Reformation doctrine in some circles has been to separate faith from social action and even to be suspicious that social action is somehow justification by works creeping in by the back door.

'Let your light shine before men, that they may see your good deeds.' Notice Jesus is saying here that people will *see good works*, not *hear sound sermons*. The message from Jesus is that faith *works*. Works matter because *true* faith is expressed in works.

Sadly, the issue has not been without controversy, and evangelicals in Britain appear to have suffered a collective case of amnesia with regard to this truth for a few generations.

Is social action evangelism?

In July 1974 the First International Congress on World Evangelisation was held in Lausanne, Switzerland. Known as the 'Lausanne Congress', it was a global conference on evangelism, called by Billy Graham and attended by over 4,000 evangelical leaders and theologians from 150 countries. The conference is noted for producing the *Lausanne Covenant*, one of the most influential documents in modern evangelical Christianity. The Drafting Committee of the covenant was chaired by John Stott.

It was the *Lausanne Covenant* that first emphasized that evangelism and social action must be interrelated. Note the *Covenant's* definition of evangelism:

> To evangelise is to spread the good news that Jesus Christ died for our sins and was raised from the dead according to the Scriptures, and that as the reigning Lord he now offers the forgiveness of sins and the liberating gifts of the Spirit to all who repent and believe. *Our Christian presence in the world is indispensable to evangelism*, and so is that kind of dialogue whose purpose is to

> listen sensitively in order to understand. But evangelism itself is the proclamation of the historical, biblical Christ as Saviour and Lord, with a view to persuading people to come to him personally and so be reconciled to God. . . . The results of evangelism include obedience to Christ, incorporation into his Church and *responsible service in the world.*[5]

While the definition is at pains to point out that evangelism itself is verbal proclamation, the document states that the social outworking of the gospel is inseparable from it – a radical statement in the evangelical circles of thirty-five years ago!

The *Covenant* goes further in repenting of evangelicalism's recent social inertia:

> Here too we express penitence both for our neglect and for having sometimes regarded evangelism and social concern as mutually exclusive. Although reconciliation with man is not reconciliation with God, nor is social action evangelism, nor is political liberation salvation, nevertheless we affirm that evangelism and socio-political involvement are both part of our Christian duty.[6]

In 1982, the Grand Rapids summit report, *Evangelism and Social Responsibility*, took this a step further by concluding that the two should be seen as partners, like the 'two wings of a bird'.

This was the position eventually adopted by John Stott. In his book, *Christian Mission in the Modern World*, he addresses the relationship between evangelism and social concern. He argues that there have been three positions in relating evangelism and social concern:

1. Social action as a *means* to evangelism. Stott writes:

> In this case evangelism and the winning of converts are the primary ends in view, but social action is a useful preliminary, an effective means to these ends. In its most blatant form this makes social work (whether food, medicine, or education) the sugar on the pill, the bait on the hook, while in its best form it gives to the Gospel a credibility it would otherwise lack. In either case the smell of hypocrisy hangs round our philanthropy. A frankly ulterior motive impels us to engage in it.[7]

2. Social action as a *manifestation* of evangelism. He writes:

> In this case philanthropy is not attached to evangelism rather artificially from the outside, but grows out of it as its natural expression. One might almost say that social action becomes the 'sacrament' of evangelism, for it makes the message significantly visible.[8]

3. Social action is a *partner* of evangelism. He writes:

> As partners the two belong to each other and yet are independent of each other. Each stands on its own feet in its own right alongside each other. Neither is a means to the other, or even a manifestation of the other. For each is an end in itself.[9]

This third position is the one advocated by Stott. Others have not settled neatly on any of these models.

Vinoth Ramachandra, Secretary for Dialogue and Social Engagement of the International Fellowship of Evangelical Students, developed the concept of holistic mission even further in his essay, 'What is Integral Mission?' He states:

> When Jesus was asked to sum up what God required of us, he did not answer in terms of either a set of 'projects' to be performed or a set of doctrines to believe. Instead we are called to love God with our whole being, and to love our neighbour the same way we love ourselves.[10]

Similarly, Tim Keller, in his book, *Ministries of Mercy: The Call of the Jericho Road*, argues:

> Word and deed, mercy and evangelism are inseparable, existing in a 'symbiotic,' interdependent relationship. If there is one thing we must conclude from all that we have explored up to this point, it is that word and deed are inextricably united and inseparable.[11]

Keller critiques John Stott's position, saying:

> We can recognize that Stott is seeking to avoid what we also argued against – calling social concern a means to an end. But to say in turn that the ministry of mercy can stand on its own and is an end in itself may pave the way for social concern that is divorced from the preaching of the gospel. This must never happen. Such deed ministry, even with a Christian motivation, cannot spread the kingdom of God. In no way can we say evangelism and social concern are 'independent.' They are interdependent equals.[12]

Keller proposes a different approach, what he calls a 'single-end' model:

> The proper model is not to see mercy as the means to evangelism, or to see mercy and evangelism as independent

> ends, but to see both word and deed, evangelism and mercy, as means to the single end of the spread of the kingdom of God. To say that social concern could be done independently of evangelism is to cut mercy loose from kingdom endeavour. It must then wither. To say that evangelism can be done without also doing social concern is to forget that our goal is not individual 'decisions,' but the bringing of all life and creation under the lordship of Christ, the kingdom of God.[13]

Not only does he reject social action as a *means* to evangelism (as in definition 1. above) and a *partner* of evangelism (as in 3.), but also as a *manifestation* of evangelism (as in 2.). For Keller, evangelism and social action are not synonymous but two inseparable callings moving toward the single unstoppable end: the establishment of the kingdom of God. It appears to me that this holistic kingdom model does the greatest justice to the complexity of the biblical data.

Are we called to social activism?

So the vast majority of Christians believe social *action* is part of the gospel package. But what about social *activism* – getting involved in the fallen structures of the world to challenge injustice and bring about a new world order?

Evangelism and Social Responsibility was the document that emerged from the International Consultation on the Relationship between Evangelism and Social Responsibility, which convened at Grand Rapids, Michigan, in June 1982. It was produced by the drafting committee, under the chairmanship of John Stott, like the *Lausanne Covenant* eight years before. This document went further than *Lausanne* in connecting social deprivation to inherent sinful human structures:

> We are appalled to know that about 800 million people, or one-fifth of the human race, are destitute, lacking the basic necessities for survival, and that thousands of them die of starvation every day. Many more millions are without adequate shelter and clothing, without clean water and health care, without opportunities for education and employment, and are condemned to eke out a miserable existence without the possibility of self-improvement for themselves or their families. They can only be described as 'oppressed' by the gross economic inequality from which they suffer and the diverse economic systems which cause and perpetuate it.
>
> The oppression of others is political. They are denied fundamental human rights by totalitarian regimes of the extreme left or right, while if they protest they are imprisoned without trial, tortured, and killed. Yet others suffer discrimination on account of their race or sex. And all of us are oppressed by global problems which seem to defy solution – conditions of overpopulation and famine, the exploitation of non-renewable resources of energy, the spoliation of the environment, community violence, war, and the ever-present threat of a nuclear holocaust.[14]

The report drew a distinction between what it called *social service* (relieving human need, philanthropic activity, seeking to minister to individuals and families, works of mercy) and *social action* (removing the causes of human need, direct political and economic activity, seeking to transform the structures of society, the quest for justice).

Radically, it concluded by stating that both were biblical and necessary and it ended with a clarion call to involvement – to be *the salt of the earth*:

> Yet we cannot stop with verbal proclamation. In addition to worldwide evangelization, the people of God should become deeply involved in relief, aid, development and the quest for justice and peace.[15]

The document notes that this is controversial, as many evangelicals did not (and still don't) believe in this second kind of social concern (activism), fearing that the church will become politicized and stray away from its gospel mandate. However, the document is uncompromising:

> Whenever the Word of God speaks clearly, the church must speak clearly also, as for example did the German Confessing Church in the Barmen Declaration of 1934, and the Norwegian Church while Norway was under German occupation in World War II. If such speech is condemned as political, we need to remember that silence would be political, too. We cannot avoid taking sides.[16]

In the autumn of 2007, while on a ministry trip to Nigeria, I went to preach at a church in the city of Jos. Fifty per cent of the country is Muslim, concentrated in the north, while 40 per cent of the population is Christian, concentrated in the south. Jos, situated in central Nigeria, is a flashpoint for violence between the two groups. As I sat in Pastor Emmanuel's office after preaching at his church, he told me of an outbreak of violence six years before, when thousands were slaughtered. It was so bad that he had to step over corpses to get into his church on the Sunday. The only reason this was not an international story is that it happened in mid September 2001 and was eclipsed by the events of 9/11.

Emmanuel shared with me one story from this time when the violence was escalating out of control. Some

Christians he knew made some makeshift fire-bombs and went to the local mosque to burn it to the ground in retaliation. Having heard of their plan, Emmanuel went to the mosque, stood inside and shouted out to the mob: 'If you are going to burn this down you are going to have to kill me!' One by one they threw down their weapons.

When I heard this I was very moved. Here was a man who didn't just *preach* good news, he *was* good news. Emmanuel knew that faith without works was not true faith. He knew that the outworking of the gospel meant seeking justice – even for his enemies – and pursuing peace for the common good.

Works are deeply evangelistic

> The church says the earth is flat, but I know that it is round, for I have seen the shadow on the moon, and I have more faith in a shadow than in the church.[17]

So wrote the Portuguese explorer, Ferdinand Magellan (1480–1521), in the sixteenth century. Cynicism towards the church and what it teaches is nothing new, nor is the sad fact that many Christians fail to be lights in the world and therefore fail to challenge the lack of faith in watching sceptics. However, Jesus said, 'Let your light shine before men, that they may see your good deeds and praise your Father in heaven.'

Good deeds are evangelistic – they will result in people coming to faith and worshipping the one true God! Bill Hybels has stated, 'The local church is the hope of the world.' It is amazing how, when the church is fulfilling her God-ordained calling, she is a source of hope in a hope-less world.

I recently went to preach at one of the churches I've been serving in Penzance, Cornwall. I chatted to Sue, an older woman who has been part of the church there for several years. I asked her how she came to faith. Becoming a Christian had quite literally changed her life. She had been an alcoholic, and when she received Christ she tipped her booze down the sink and has not had a drink since.

But what had led her to this point? She was walking through Penzance one Saturday morning and stumbled across the church doing a complimentary shoe-shine in the town square. She couldn't get her head around this random act of kindness – in particular, the pastor himself was on his knees shining people's shoes. This *demonstration* of the good news connected her to the church, and she embarked on an Alpha course and eventually became a Christian. Good works are evangelistic.

Matthew Parris recently penned a fascinating article in *The Times* newspaper, entitled 'As an atheist, I truly believe Africa needs God'. The article was about a recent trip he had made to his boyhood home of Malawi. He writes:

> Now a confirmed atheist, I've become convinced of the enormous contribution that Christian evangelism makes in Africa: sharply distinct from the work of secular NGOs, government projects and international aid efforts. These alone will not do. Education and training alone will not do. In Africa Christianity changes people's hearts. It brings a spiritual transformation. The rebirth is real . . .
>
> I noticed that a handful of the most impressive African members of the Pump Aid team . . . were, privately, strong Christians. 'Privately' because the charity is entirely secular and I never heard any of its team so

> much as mention religion while working in the villages. But I picked up the Christian references in our conversations. One, I saw, was studying a devotional textbook in the car. One, on Sunday, went off to church at dawn for a two-hour service.
>
> It would suit me to believe that their honesty, diligence and optimism in their work was unconnected with personal faith. Their work was secular, but surely affected by what they were.[18]

What I love about this is Parris going out of his way to let us know these Christians were not preachy. Despite this, it's as if they couldn't hide who they were. Sound familiar? 'A city on a hill cannot be hidden. Neither do people light a lamp and put it under a bowl. Instead they put it on its stand, and it gives light to everyone in the house.'

Now Parris is still an atheist but it is amazing that his observation is that Christianity *works* – the people he encountered with real character were people of real faith.

True faith expresses itself in godly action, and that is deeply evangelistic.

Chapter 11

Ministering in the Miraculous
Signs and wonders in evangelism

Roy Todd

> Miracles are a retelling in small letters of the very same story, which is written across the whole world in letters too large for some of us to see.
>
> C. S. Lewis[1]

Miracles – or to give them another name, signs of the kingdom of God – have always had the power to get people to sit up and take notice. They may be stating the obvious, but as C. S. Lewis astutely observed, many people are blind to the obvious so need something to get their attention. We might think miracles are not very British but they are very biblical.

Miracles were an intrinsic part of Jesus' evangelistic ministry. He healed incurable diseases, raised dead people back to life, turned water into fine wine, fed over 5,000 people using just five loaves and two fish, released those oppressed by demonic possession . . . and the list could go on.

If the amount of space an author takes to write about a particular subject is an indication of its importance, then the writers of the Gospels must have viewed miracles as highly significant. Matthew devotes 44 per cent of his Gospel to Jesus' miracles, Mark 29 per cent, Luke 30 per cent and John 30 per cent. Luke continues to write about signs and wonders in the early church, with 27 per cent of the entire Book of Acts focusing on charismatic and out-of-the-ordinary activity.

The realm of the miraculous

Jesus himself instructed the church to expect miraculous accompaniments to their proclamation of the good news. In Mark 16:17–20, Jesus declares that five 'signs' follow those 'who believe':

> '. . . And these signs will accompany those who believe: In my name they will drive out demons; they will speak in new tongues; they will pick up snakes with their hands; and when they drink deadly poison, it will not hurt them at all; they will place their hands on sick people, and they will get well.'
>
> After the Lord Jesus had spoken to them, he was taken up into heaven and he sat at the right hand of God. Then the disciples went out and preached everywhere, and the Lord worked with them and confirmed his word by the signs that accompanied it (NIV).

Amazing though it is, it's unlikely that this list is exhaustive – however, it does give examples of the types of miraculous signs that can be expected. Miracles are *signs of the kingdom* that point to something beyond themselves.

In the list below (taken from Mark 16:17–20) we can see how a particular sign in the ministry of the believer points beyond itself to the ushering in of the kingdom that Jesus came to accomplish:

- *Casting out demons*: signs of Christ's pre-eminence.
- *Speaking in new tongues*: signs of Christ's power.
- *Picking up snakes*: signs of Christ's protection.
- *Drinking deadly poison and not being harmed*: signs of Christ's preservation.
- *Placing hands on sick people so they can recover*: signs of Christ's provision.

The purpose of signs and wonders is *to make people wonder*. They still occur today – and they're just as relevant today as they were in Bible times. I can best say what I wish to communicate about the place of signs in contemporary evangelism by sharing my own journey of how I came to minister in the miraculous.

My story: Surprised by spiritual power

My own journey into the miraculous certainly wasn't planned by me. It wasn't something I yearned for or sought after. In fact, to this day, it still amazes me that I even find myself writing or speaking about signs and wonders – let alone ministering in them. I guess that's God for you – he is truly the God of surprises.

It's not that there was a time in my life when I *didn't* believe in miracles. The truth is that I've always believed in them. Brought up in a Spirit-filled church in Belfast where faith was strong and the Bible taken seriously, I really had no choice but to believe. Yet when I started out as an evangelist, I never thought miracles would play a major part in my ministry. I'm a communicator. I always thought God would merely use my preaching as the means by which people would be drawn to personal faith. The truth is, I really wanted to be like my hero, Billy Graham. Miracles were never a feature of his ministry – yet millions of people became Christians at his meetings.

But God had other ideas for me. Have you ever noticed that God often takes you in the direction you least expect?

Little did I realize then that miracles would actually become a huge accompaniment to my ministry. Even today, whether I intentionally pray for people or not in events where I'm invited to speak, it's not uncommon for people to come to me afterwards and say things like, 'God healed me as you were speaking today.' I often wonder why that is. I guess it's partly because their faith has been built up as they've listened to the Bible. There's also got to be the involvement of personal expectancy too. But the most solid conclusion I always make is that it's God simply doing what God does – and using me as a channel through which to do it.

'So when did you begin to see miracles happen in your ministry?' That's a question I'm often asked. Sometimes people anticipate a dramatic answer involving stories about Isaiah-like encounters with God, life-after-death experiences, angelic visitations . . . and the rest. But looking back, the first major miracle I ever witnessed involved none of those things.

As a wet-behind-the-ears twenty-one-year-old evangelist who had launched out in ministry just over a year before, it was normal for me to preach to small congregations with as few as five people and rarely more than fifty. So you can imagine my reaction when, one day, I received an invitation to be the guest speaker at an event in the north-east of England at which 300 people would gather! I gladly accepted the invitation and proceeded to prepare a brand-new sermon especially for the occasion (I had three usable sermons up to that point). I even rehearsed it a number of times in front of a mirror so I would get it just right on the night!

After weeks of waiting, the day of the *big* meeting finally came. I drove to the venue feeling both excited and nervous at the same time. However, when I arrived and saw a packed car park, nervousness became my predominant emotion, as I was now on the verge of addressing the largest congregation I'd ever spoken to in my life.

I had no idea that this meeting would take an unexpected twist – and one that would literally change the course of my ministry. At 7 p.m. the service commenced. It began optimistically enough, but after the first few songs, it started to drag on. The format was roughly five fast songs, followed by five slow songs, followed by another fast song (for the offering – cheerful giving and all that), followed by some slow songs, some slower songs and then the slowest songs. At this point, it was as if the meeting became transfixed into a state of slow motion, and I desperately wanted to press a 'fast forward' button to speed the proceedings up. The worship time just went on and on and on . . . and then, when it looked like it might finish . . . it went on again.

Meanwhile, I felt concerned in case people got bored and left early, thus missing the wonderful new sermon I'd prepared especially for them! After all, the reason why they'd come was to hear me preach, right? Well, that's what I thought.

At around 9 p.m. the elderly pastor leading the service eventually stood up on the platform to introduce me. In his strong Geordie accent he said, 'We 'ave a young man as our guest speaka this evenin'. His name is . . . ahhhh . . . ohhhhh . . .' Then he stopped, looked at me from the platform and publicly asked, 'What's ya name, son?'

In a James Bond-esque moment, I made my dramatic introduction to the Christian world as I announced, 'My name's Todd . . . Roy Todd.'

However, the poignancy of the moment was completely lost as the pastor put his hand to his ear, positioned it like a satellite dish towards me and said in almost interrogatory fashion, 'Speak up, son – I canna hear ya!'

This time, I dispensed with the histrionics, simply shouting, 'Roy Todd!'

'Ah yes . . .' he said. 'We 'ave a young man called Roy Todd. He 'as come all the way from Ireland – especially to speak to us tonight. [I'd actually been resident in England for three years at that point.] Let's give him a very special welcome as he comes to the platform.'

As I approached the stage, the welcome of the 300-strong congregation was underwhelming, to say the least, as only about three of them joined in the applause. I felt somewhat deflated, as I could never have imagined Billy Graham receiving an introduction like that! I climbed the three steps up to the platform and walked across to the lectern in the centre. I began by giving some customary words of thanks to the pastor, introduced myself to the people and then proceeded to preach my shiny new sermon with its three major points, each containing six sub-points.

After preaching for around twenty-five minutes, I drew to a close and gave an appeal for those who wanted to become Christians. Four people responded. Feeling encouraged by this, I prayed a simple prayer for the four respondents, after which I picked up my sermon notes, vacated the platform and happily walked back to my seat on the front row – somewhat relieved that my job was now done. But little did I know that my night had only just begun!

Out of the comfort zone

The elderly pastor left his seat and made his way over to where I was sitting. With as much discretion as a polar bear suffering from a headache, he loudly whispered, 'Why are ya sittin' down?'

I replied, 'What do you mean?'

He said, 'You 'aven't finished yet.'

I responded, 'I have finished.'

'No, you 'aven't!' he said with a stern voice. 'You've yet to pray for tha people to receive miracles!'

Using all the diplomacy I could possibly muster, I attempted to reason with the old man of God – but to no avail. I whispered, 'Well . . . I don't really do that kind of thing, you see . . .'

Before I could utter another word, he interrupted me: 'Well, ya better do it tonight! We've advertised that ya will pray for people to receive miracles! Do ya really think these people came just to hear ya preach? Get on to that platform and get on with it!'

At this point, I broke into a cold sweat as I realized I was left with little choice but to return to the platform. Shaking from head to foot, I stood up and began to walk towards the stage. Although it was only a matter of a few metres, at the time it felt like the longest walk I'd ever taken in my life. Twenty-one years of living flashed right before my eyes as I made my way in fear and trepidation. The walk to the platform twenty-five minutes earlier had been relatively easy – if a little nerve-racking. At least then I had a good idea of what was going to happen next. But this time, it was completely different. I was now entering uncharted territory for which I was totally unprepared. I felt totally out of my comfort zone and literally had no idea how this would all pan out!

I climbed the three steps up to the platform, walked over to the lectern and nervously looked out over the congregation. For a few agonizing moments, my mind went totally blank and I really didn't know what to say next. The spectacle of a preacher lost for words sent the bemused audience into a confused silence – leaving them wondering what was going on. But after what seemed like a lifetime, I somehow managed to gather my thoughts and remembered what the elderly pastor had told me to do. I spoke gently and quietly into the microphone as I timidly announced, 'Ah . . . by the way . . . if anyone would like prayer, please come forward.'

At first, it looked as if I may have got away with it, as no one seemed to respond. But my relief was short lived as, slowly but surely, sounds of footsteps began coming my way. There were only a few to begin with – but that soon changed as literally half the congregation made their way to the front. At this point, I felt I needed prayer for healing myself as I was convinced I was just about to have a panic attack!

I stood silently and looked out over a sea of faces, all coming in my direction. I distinctly remember feeling completely daunted by the idea that these people were actually expecting the power of God to be manifested through little me! Convinced they would be disappointed, I quickly formed an exit strategy in my mind, glancing to see where the nearest fire exit was so I could make a quick get-away in the likely event of an emergency!

As the crowd stood at the front, a middle-aged woman among them caught my eye. She was leaning on a walking-frame and was bent over in great pain. I later learned that she had major spinal problems, which would eventually confine her to a wheelchair. I don't know why, but I decided to pray for her first. I came off the stage, made my way over to her and laid my hands on her head. The first words of my prayer were, 'Lord, it would be wonderful if this lady could be healed.' The next line included a little King James English, which always tends to have the effect of making prayers sound more spiritual: 'Lord, if it be thy will – thou canst heal thy servant.' Nice words – but there really wasn't a lot of faith going on.

Surprised by the sovereignty of God

Suddenly, in the middle of my gentle prayer, God spoke to me. It wasn't an audible voice – but an unmistakable still, small voice that was clear as clear can be. I know that's a strong statement – but there simply is no other way of describing it. The voice said to me, 'Take this woman's walking-frame away!' It was so distinct and profound that I felt totally compelled to obey it. You may wonder why I'm so sure this was God speaking. The answer is simple – I really would *never* have told myself to do that!

So I proceeded to act on what I had heard God tell me to do. I removed the walking-frame on which the woman was leaning and set it to the side. Meanwhile, she (now without support) lost her balance and nearly fell over. I grabbed hold of her just in the nick of time and held on to her. At this point, I would love to tell you that she got instantly healed. But that's not what happened. That would be too easy – and besides, God likes to make life interesting for us, don't you think? The truth is that after I removed the walking-frame, nothing happened for well over one minute. Of course, when you're standing in front of a crowd who are focusing intensely on you, one minute is a very long time. During this period, the woman held firmly on to me – and if I'm honest, I gripped tightly on to her for dear life too. I remember watching her curious eyes staring at me inquisitively as if to say, 'What are you going to do next?' I then looked out at the congregation, who also gazed at me with pondering eyes asking, 'What is he going to do next?'

Meanwhile, the elderly pastor stood behind me on the platform. I thought it might be a good idea to give him a quick glance – thinking he would give me a look of encouragement and approval. But I was not encouraged when I turned around and saw him staring intensely back at me with one eye open and one eye shut. It was clear what he was thinking: 'If this works, you will be back. If this doesn't work, you'll need a walking-frame yourself by the time I finish with you!'

After one minute of absolute nothingness, something shocking and mind-boggling occurred right before my eyes. The woman for whom I was praying suddenly jolted. Then her bent-over body began to slowly straighten up until she was completely upright. Quietly, she turned around, faced in the opposite direction from me and began to walk. It was a slow pace at first but she got faster and faster and faster – until she began to run all around the auditorium. Members of the congregation began to clap their hands and cheer at the sight of the woman, now jumping and leaping for joy. She had been healed – just like that!

Meanwhile, I was in a kind of dazed state. The roller-coaster of emotions I'd just experienced had worn me out and I was worried I might be hallucinating! But I wasn't. With my own eyes, I had witnessed something that was nothing short of a miracle. One minute, she was bent over in agony and dependent on a walking-frame – the next, she was pain-free and no longer needing any support. It truly was astonishing.

At the end of the service, the elderly pastor came to me with his diary already open, wanting to arrange my next visit. After we agreed the date, he smiled and said, 'I look forward to seeing ya next time, then!' – words I hadn't expected to hear!

We need to exercise faith

Thus began my journey into the miraculous. From that night, God birthed a passion in my heart to *believe* for people to experience miracles today. I decided that from then on, I would pray for people at every church where I was invited to speak. And that's exactly what I've done.

God wants us not to just believe *in* miracles but to believe him *for* them. We need to exercise our faith. The journey God took me on brought me to the point where I exercised faith in him – faith that I would witness signs accompanying the ministry of the word.

Perhaps I was a little naive at times, especially as some churches were not used to having visiting speakers lay hands on members of the congregation! But no one ever objected. More to the point – the results spoke for themselves. Story after story emerged of people receiving miracles as a result of prayer.

The anointing will open doors for you

Word began to spread and invitations came flooding in from all over the UK, asking me to speak at evangelistic events where people could receive prayer for miracles. I accepted all of them. It really didn't matter to me whether they were large or small churches. I was just delighted to have the opportunity of proclaiming the good news of Jesus Christ and praying for people to experience his miraculous power.

Stories of healing became front-page news in some of the towns and cities I visited. I even made a number of appearances on local TV and radio stations, giving interviews that were received very favourably. I was honoured to address some significant Christian conferences, speaking on the theme of signs and wonders. Doors also began to open for me to preach at huge meetings in different parts of the world – including Africa and Asia. Most importantly of all, more and more unchurched people attended the events where I was invited to speak in the UK, sometimes making up about 70 per cent of the entire audience! Some came out of curiosity, others because of scepticism, and still more because of personal circumstances. But for whatever reason they came, many of them left 'ransomed, healed, restored, forgiven'.

Over a decade later, the ministry continues to grow from strength to strength. Many thousands of unchurched people are being impacted each year through events I'm honoured to lead. The passion that was first birthed in my heart over ten years ago grows stronger every day and I really believe the best is still to come. I am absolutely convinced that nothing is impossible with God. It's my God-given mission in life to inspire people to personal faith in Christ by helping them experience the reality of who he is today.

Ministering in the miraculous: the need of the hour

While British and European culture is generally disinterested in and cynical of dry, institutional Christianity, I've found that the vast majority of unchurched people I have spoken with are open to God or at least to the spiritual dimension to life. They are hungry for wholeness. They are longing for fulfilment. They are desperate for reality.

George Harrison, member of the Beatles, was a spiritual seeker all his life. He once stated: 'The purpose in life is to find out who am I, why am I here and where am I going – that's what we all need answering.'

What he was saying is that most people's life quest is to discover identity, purpose and destiny. He was right: it's just that so many people seek all the *right* things in all the *wrong* places. Yet in Christianity lies the answer: Jesus Christ. Not a religion but a person.

He offers reality, fulfilment and wholeness. In him we find identity, purpose and destiny. Surely the multitudes flocked to Jesus because they saw someone who was authentic, offering genuine solutions to their real needs. Christ's message has not changed. He is the same yesterday, today and forever!

In an age that is closed to *organized religion* but open to the *spiritual*, the church needs to rediscover its God-given mandate to *minister in the miraculous*. To do so is to demonstrate signs to make people wonder – so that they may be shaken from their doubts and disbelief and come in awe and wonder to the God of wonder, who longs to know them and restore them into an eternal friendship with himself.

Chapter 12

Preaching the Full Gospel
Healing in evangelism

Don Egan

> Healing . . . it is not the whole Gospel, nor the chief part of it, but it is a part, and in its due subordination to the whole, it will prove, like the Gospel itself, the power of God unto everyone that believeth.
>
> A. B. Simpson (1843–1919),
> Founder of the Christian Missionary Alliance[1]

Healing is an integral part of the good news of Jesus Christ. Not that you'd know that from observing most circles of the church. All too often either healing is not believed in or it is viewed as a scary optional extra. Despite the evidence of Scripture, tradition and present-day experience, there remain churches that are against healing.

A friend of mine applied to be the vicar of a church in the London area. At the interview a woman who ran the prayer team found out he was a charismatic and said curtly, 'We don't want that kind of thing here.' My friend enquired what she meant, and she explained: 'speaking in tongues and healing'. When he asked if the prayer team prayed for the sick at the end of the services, she responded, 'Yes, but we don't expect people to get healed.' He shared what the woman had said at the formal interview and said to the panel, 'If that lady's view is representative of a large number in the church, I urge you not to appoint me.' They didn't!

Even churches that believe in and practise healing seem embarrassed by the ministry of healing. It's often done at the end of the service or relegated to a side chapel or over to one side of the church. It's actually part of the main event, not an optional extra for those who like that kind of thing. Healing ministry should really be done immediately after the preaching of the word, right in the main body of the church. It should not be sidelined, done behind closed doors, rushed or apologized for.

Healing is as integral to the gospel as the cross and resurrection. It is not an optional extra. It's just that some people, who want to avoid controversy, promote a 'good news lite' version of the gospel, which, frankly, lacks power. Christianity is far more than a cerebral assent to certain doctrines. In 1 Corinthians 2:4 Paul writes: 'My message and my preaching were not with wise and persuasive words, but with a demonstration of the Spirit's power' (NIV).

The gospel of Jesus is a combination of truth and power. Some people come to Christ through an encounter with the *truth*. Others have an encounter with the *power* of God.

A big factor in me becoming a Christian was being exposed to the power of God in healing today. I was searching for God as a young man. I read the Gospels and some religious tracts. Then I was in a pub with a friend of mine when he said, 'Isn't Jesus wonderful?' It was a conversation stopper, but I was fascinated. He told me how, in church the previous Sunday, the vicar had told the people that Jesus had taught his followers to lay hands on the sick and pray for them. There was a woman, called Hilda, in the church who had Parkinson's Disease. A few people had joined the vicar and laid hands on Hilda and prayed for her healing. By Tuesday that week, the doctor confirmed that Hilda was free from Parkinson's Disease.

The story staggered me. I couldn't believe anyone would get healed in church. When I'd gone to church for Parade Sunday, when I was in the Cubs, it was so bleak and boring that I thought it more likely someone would keel over and die in church! In fact, I saw a big plaque on the wall of the church with a long list of names on it. It said that these were the names of those who had 'died in the services'. I wondered if it was the morning or the evening services!

Healing is part of apostolic Christianity

Our pattern for evangelism, however modern or on-the-edge we may be, must have its roots in the life of Jesus Christ. He *is* the gospel, the good news. During his three-year ministry he called people to himself. He trained them. They were known as *disciples* – literally, followers – like an apprentice or pupil. Later on, he began to take these disciples and send them out as *apostles* (literally, *ones who are sent*) to act on his behalf.

In Matthew 10:1–2 it is interesting to note what changes a *disciple* (one who follows) into an *apostle* (one who is sent):

> He called his twelve disciples to him and gave them authority to drive out evil spirits and to heal every disease and sickness. These are the names of the twelve *apostles* . . . (NIV).

In the first verse, he calls *disciples*. Then he gives them *authority* (in the Greek, *exousia* – literally: power, authority, strength) to 'drive out evil spirits' and to 'heal every disease and sickness'.

Then in the second verse, they are referred to as *apostles* sent by God *with power and authority*. Jesus didn't teach them a 'knowing God in three simple steps' formula but gave the disciples three building-blocks. They were told to *preach, heal, and drive out demons*. He enrolled his disciples in a PhD programme: they were to Preach, Heal and Deliver.

This is the authentic apostolic gospel. This reflects the fully orbed gospel so lacking in the church today – the message that *Jesus saves, Jesus heals and Jesus delivers*!

Jesus and the apostles never go looking for demons, they only deal with them when they manifest or interfere with the work of the gospel (Acts 16:17–18). So the normal presentation of the gospel was preaching and healing and deliverance. Healing and miracles are like the words through the centre of a stick of rock. Slice the gospel anywhere and inside you'll find healing and miracles: a glimpse of the kingdom on earth. 'Heal the sick who are there and tell them, "The kingdom of God is near you"' (Luke 10:9 NIV).

It has always been so. Throughout the ages, the spread of the gospel has often been accompanied by the work of divine healing. For example, in his book, *The Conversion of Europe*, Richard Fletcher writes about Aredius, in Gaul, who was attached to the court of King Theudebert (534–48). He was recruited by Bishop Nicetius of Trier and returned later to Limosin, dedicating his life to the service of God. We are told: 'The sick flocked to him and he restored them to health by laying on of hands with the sign of the cross.'[2]

So what about today?

Healing is God's will for his church today

Years ago, I was preaching at a conference in Rwanda. As I closed my message, we prayed for the sick. It was done African style – we all prayed at once. As we did, an old woman in the crowd began shouting and pointing at me. I thought she was accusing me of something. But the interpreter smiled. 'No,' he said. 'She is telling everyone that she has been listening to you speak at the conference these last few days, but she didn't know you were a white man, because she's been blind for twelve years. But as we were praying her eyes opened and she could see your face and the faces of her friends.'

Another girl jumped up on the platform, also telling the crowd how her eyesight had been restored as we prayed. An old woman began bending over and touching her toes, explaining that her crippling abdominal pain had just been healed. From that day, all heaven seemed to break loose in our meetings in Africa.

Once I went to speak to thirty clergymen in a remote village, but 1,500 people turned up to hear me. Due to the numbers, we had the meetings outside the church and every evening many people gave their lives to Jesus and many were healed. A man near the back did a little dance. He was telling everyone that four men had carried him to the meeting because he couldn't walk, but when I prayed for the crowd the night before, he had been healed.

In village after village across Rwanda I saw dramatic healings everywhere I preached. Crutches were thrown away, the blind received their sight, the deaf heard and the lame walked. Pain was dissipated and disease disappeared. The kingdom of God was glimpsed on earth. The ancient prayer we have prayed for so long – 'Your kingdom come, your will be done, on earth as in heaven' – was manifestly answered.

But what about here in the UK, I hear you say? Do such things happen *here* today?

Open doors to seeing God heal today: Faith and freedom

Some years ago I was returning from Rwanda after one of the most amazing weeks in my life. In just one week over 2,000 people had committed their lives to Jesus Christ. Many others had been healed and set free from pain and sickness. A seasoned and well-known alcoholic in the village received Jesus, sobered up and was delivered of his addiction (he has never touched alcohol since).

As the plane touched down at Heathrow, I asked God, 'Why do we not see these things in the UK?' Immediately, I heard the still, small voice of God: 'You will never see such things in the UK and in your ministry, because you don't expect me to do anything in your UK meetings, and you don't ever give me space to work.' Ouch! I repented right there on the plane. 'Lord, the very next time I am asked to speak about healing in the UK, I will go expecting you to heal, and I will give you space and time to work.'

Lack of expectation is lack of *faith*. Even to have faith and not step out in it is an inhibitor. I needed to have faith and create space – I had to give God the *freedom* to move in my ministry.

A few weeks later, I was driving through heavy rain and howling gales to a little village Anglican church in East Anglia. It was a bleak night. The service I was asked to speak at was a 1662 *Book of Common Prayer* Evensong, during which they made space for prayer for healing. A more extreme cultural contrast with my services in Rwanda would be hard to find!

The congregation was usually small for this service but I had agreed to go nonetheless. I noticed in the church magazine that it had been advertised as 'Evensnog', which I thought might bring a few extra people! It didn't appear to.

I asked the vicar if any of the thirty or so people gathered would come forward for prayer. 'One or two, usually,' he replied.

'Well, Lord, how are you going to do anything here?' I thought. I kept my two promises to God. First, against all the odds, I strangely *expected* him to do *something*. Second, I was determined to give him space to work.

I preached about the paralysed man let down through the roof by his four friends. I spoke about the many who hindered, the few who helped and the One who healed. At the end of my message, all but two of the congregation came forward for prayer. In such an inauspicious setting, there were two dramatic healings that night.

The first was Penny. It was a miracle in itself that she was even there – she suffered from Seasonal Affected Disorder (SAD), and from October to April every year she was severely depressed and hardly left her house. Some days she couldn't even get out of bed, she felt so low. Her only partial relief came from sitting in front of a special light-box for hours at a time. I laid hands on Penny's head and started to pray and quoted Romans 12:2: 'Be transformed by the renewing of your mind.'

As soon as I said that, Penny suddenly declared, 'I'm healed!' I have to say, in all honesty I didn't believe her. I mean, I hadn't prayed *properly* yet, and such an outburst of enthusiasm seemed a bit out of place in this rural, Church of England parish.

She wrote to me that week about how her life had been completely transformed by the healing she received. Her grown-up son also had the same disorder and he was set free the following Thursday, as he was reading his Bible. Then her grandson, who was also displaying signs of the affliction, was healed. I met Penny several times after that and the problem never recurred.

The second notable miracle was with a woman called Louise whose young daughter had suddenly become aggressive and verbally abusive to her and her husband and was refusing to go to school. It was about eight o'clock when I prayed with Louise. Her husband and daughter were not present at the service but had stayed at home. I prayed with Louise and really felt God tell me that her daughter had a spirit of fear on her. So we rebuked and bound that spirit of fear as I laid hands on Louise as a point of contact with her daughter.

Louise got in touch with me later in the week. She got home on Sunday night and her husband immediately said, 'Something strange happened at eight o'clock.' He explained that their daughter had a complete character change and became peaceful. The next morning, Louise was seeing her husband off to work at the front door. They heard a little voice behind them saying, 'Good morning, Mummy and Daddy.' It was their daughter, sitting on the stairs, dressed and ready for school. It changed their lives.

I was praying for the sick at a mission meeting in Middlesex. An old woman was preparing to have three cancerous lumps removed from her spine. I prayed with her and cursed the lumps and told them to shrivel up and die – I'd preached about speaking to mountains and telling them to be removed. When the doctors operated two days later, they were surprised to find that two of the lumps had disappeared and the third was a fraction of its previous size.

Recently, I was praying for the sick in a healing service at a church in Blackpool. Many came forward for prayer. Among them was an elderly woman who had lost much of her sight many years before. She had imagined how people looked from the sound of their voice because she couldn't see anyone's face. As she left the church that night she thought she saw someone's face, which was unusual. The following Sunday she stood up in church and told how, over the week, her eyesight had gradually returned. She'd even read twenty pages of my book on healing, when normally she would really struggle to read even a paragraph of anything.

At a meeting in Surrey, I prayed for a man who had injured his knee while preparing for a cycling marathon. He had arrived at church in severe pain that morning. As I took his hand and declared the word of God over him, 'By his wounds, you are healed', all the pain vanished and he was able to walk normally.

A couple who came to another such meeting were childless. The wife had a disease in her womb, which made it impossible for her to conceive. I prayed with them and declared her healing and the blessing of God on them. A year later, almost to the day, they sent me a photograph of their beautiful daughter.

When I was a little boy, I used to love a TV programme called *Stingray*. Like its sister programme *Thunderbirds*, it looks laughably dated now but it was very state of the art then! It was about a futuristic submarine crew who lived under the sea. The programme started with loud drumbeats and explosions. A security building fell into the sea. Rockets were launched. The submarine shot through an underwater scene and the announcer declared boldly, 'Anything can happen in the next half hour!' I think that phrase should be engraved above the door of every church in the land. We should always come expecting God to show up in power when we meet together.

Mark 16:20 says, 'Then the disciples went out and preached everywhere, and the Lord worked with them and confirmed his word by the signs that accompanied it' (NIV). Are you giving God the *space* (freedom) to work in your church? Do you *expect* (have faith) that God will accompany the preaching of his word with signs?

Barriers to seeing God heal today: Fear and pride

It has often been said that biblically, the opposite of faith is not doubt but *fear*. This, I believe, is the greatest impediment to seeing God heal today in the Western church. Only a minority of Christians believe God does not heal today (a view known as *cessationism*). Most Christians believe God can heal but do not see it. I believe the greatest reason for this is fear.

The great fear, in church leadership, which I hear constantly, is, 'What if nothing happens?' Those who ask that question don't know or believe their Bible. The Bible makes it clear: 'nothing is impossible with God' (Luke 1:37 NIV).

I *can't* tell you exactly *what* will happen when you pray for healing, expecting God to do something. What I *can* tell you is what will *not* happen. What will not happen is – *nothing*. Because *nothing is impossible with God*. Something has to happen.

Similarly, the presence of *pride* can be a barrier to the work of healing. Some people use the ministry of healing to validate themselves as a person, which can inhibit God's power to heal. We should avoid having people who talk about *their* healing ministry on any team. Spiritualists and psychic healers talk about *their gift*.

I do *not* have a healing ministry. I have a ministry to preach the good news and make disciples. As I do *that*, I expect God to heal. It's *his* healing ministry. It's all about him. The Holy Spirit does give gifts of healing, but we should never look to a human agency for healing but to *Jesus alone*.

Healing is deeply evangelistic

The healing ministry of Jesus was never intended simply for those inside the church. Out in the market-place of the world we should incorporate the sharing of the gospel with healing ministry. John 2:11 states about Jesus turning water into wine:

> This, the first of his miraculous signs, Jesus performed in Cana of Galilee. He thus revealed his glory, and his disciples *put their faith in him* (NIV).

The purpose of signs such as healing is the extension of the kingdom of God.

When I was working in Suffolk, I prayed with various people who came to healing services. One woman, Laura, who was not a Christian, had been blind for forty years when she came to a series of meetings. Over a period of about five weeks her eyesight was restored, improving dramatically every time we prayed. Perhaps not surprisingly, she later gave her life to Jesus. I met her in a shop after she was healed and she told me she had hung out the washing on her own for the first time. That Christmas she gave me a little present. She had been doing cross-stitch and made me a little bookmark for my Bible. It is a very simple gift but I often carry it in my Bible because people who are blind don't do cross-stitch. Only those who can see the small detail involved can do it. It serves as a permanent testimony to her healing.

Once miracles begin to happen, the gospel is gossiped without any heavy exhortation to evangelize. This is how the news of Jesus spread across the whole region where he lived. There is no cringe factor in telling the story of how someone got healed by Jesus.

People who do not believe may not turn up to hear a gospel choir or an eminent theologian. But they may well turn out for something authentically supernatural. The world is busy seeking out spiritualists, hypnotists, psychics and New Age gurus. Acupuncture and alternative therapies abound. But all these are counterfeits of the real thing. Jesus, the Son of righteousness, has risen with healing in his wings.

Let us offer this Jesus to a lost, hurting and sick world. We should pray for people to be healed on the streets, at bus stops, in hospitals and restaurants. I've prayed for people in pubs as the barman cleared up. In many ways, I find that non-Christians often get healed more easily than Christians. God is more ready to manifest his kingdom to the lost than we are to pray. Wherever we come expecting a miracle and give God space, he will manifest his power.

Let's not just be Bible-believing Christians but Bible-obeying Christians. Let's not allow our Western cynical and anti-supernaturalist culture to paralyse us into inaction. It is clear from the Scriptures that the eternal God who is the same yesterday, today and forever, saves, heals and delivers. He has not stopped, so why have we?

Let's step out in faith and pray for the sick, as Jesus commanded, so that men and women might be healed as a sign to reveal the glory of God – and seeing his glory, might come to put their faith in him.

Chapter 13

Take the Roof Off Your Thinking!
Evangelism that culturally connects

Mark Ritchie

> Sometimes we stare so long at a door that is closing that we see too late the one that is open.
>
> Alexander Graham Bell (1847–1922)[1]

As I stood in the wings, I was panicking. The theatre was full of people ready to see a one-man stand-up comedy show, and it was suddenly dawning on me that I was *that* man! I was about to boldly go . . .

My mind quickly retraced the steps of how on earth I found myself to be here. It had been an interesting journey. I am an evangelist and have always been passionate about trying to connect with unchurched people. Five years ago, I began to feel frustrated that many of the events and services I was asked to speak at were full of Christians. I talked to God, I talked to a mentor, and then I talked to God some more. I knew that this was a common problem faced by many evangelists.

Like many others, I had been invited to speak at an evangelistic event on numerous occasions, only to find that the organizers' brief for me to come and speak to an event which would be 'at least 50 per cent non-Christians' did not quite materialize. This was obvious when I asked one of the organizers on the night, 'How many guests would you say are here?' and watched as he began to squirm uncomfortably.

'Erm . . . well . . . difficult to say . . .'

'That's OK – just a rough estimate would do,' I persisted.

'Well, including those on the fringe – Bob who comes with his wife (strong woman, Freda), and Janice, who's religious but doesn't know the Lord – say nine.'

It wasn't that the event hadn't been conceived with good intentions. The charge had gone out clearly to the church: 'Only come if you bring a non-believing friend' – but when push came to shove, people had their various excuses and the event was predominantly attended by Christians.

The reasons for this are many and various but one reason is surely that people who have been Christians for a number of years get so immersed in church culture that they cease to have meaningful or deep friendships with non-Christians. Laurence Singlehurst refers to this as 'total sanctification: no non-Christian friends'.

I tired of the excuses of pastors who attempted to put a positive spin on what, in worldly terms, would be a disaster: 'Never mind, brother – it was good for the church to be reminded of the basic gospel again.' This may well be true, but God had called me to herald the message of salvation to those *outside* the church. The apostle Paul never said, 'Woe to me if I do not remind Christians of the basic gospel again.' He said, 'Woe to me if I do not preach the gospel.'

Also, it felt as if some of the evangelistic methods that churches were using were from a very old paradigm of mission and were clearly not working. Having a Cliff Richard look-alike do a medley of songs on a Saturday night, reaching a finale with the 'Millennium Prayer' when I was wheeled on to speak, didn't seem to have deep cultural resonance. Stuff like this may have worked well in its day, but it appeared stale and lacking in creativity in this new millennium. I prayed a bit more. Then I had a *holy eureka* moment.

My wife had booked us in to see a comedian at our local theatre. This man gripped hundreds of people for two hours, laughing and listening to his stories. As I sat in the theatre, God spoke to me and said, 'You can do this.'

The outcome has been that I have been touring an evangelistic one-man show around the UK, which often has audiences of up to *70 per cent* unchurched. People are laughing, and then they are crying, and ultimately, they are weighing up their lives in the light of the cross. The gospel has broken out of the church in a new and innovative way. And the events haven't only been an opportunity to engage in seeker-friendly pre-evangelism, but we have seen many come to Christ directly as a result.

I am convinced we must continue to think differently when it comes to the gospel. The gospel never changes but the cultural expression of it does, and we need to do the hard work of thinking about what it means to proclaim afresh God's good news in our own rapidly changing culture. We need a *new paradigm* for the old, old story that resonates with post-modern, post-Christian, secular Britain.

A biblical model for this new paradigm can be found in the story of the healing of the paralytic (Mark 2:1–12). Evangelism, in a nutshell, is *introducing people to Jesus*, and this is what the four stretcher-bearers are doing in this story. The story is about this bloke who was paralysed and couldn't walk, but he was desperate to see

Jesus. Because of his condition he didn't stand a chance of getting near as Jesus-mania swept the region and, wherever he went, Jesus was surrounded by the crowds. One day, when Jesus was preaching in Capernaum, there were so many people that he was hemmed into the house in which he was preaching. The bloke's mates had an idea. They risked getting a Palestinian ASBO and made a hole in the roof and lowered their friend down using a stretcher and ropes. Jesus was so impressed by this guy's determination to meet him that he forgave the man's sin and then healed him of his paralysis on the spot. The bloke got up and walked out.

I wish to share five principles that we can draw out of the story that are very relevant to pioneer evangelism.

The four friends saw a *need*

Nothing would have happened if the four friends had not grasped the dire need of their friend.

Nothing will change in our approach to evangelism if we are engaging in it to fill pews or increase the giving. The vital question is, can I see the need? Does it hurt us that we are not doing evangelism or that many of our current evangelistic programmes are not working? Does it bother you that the church is by and large failing to connect with a generation without the knowledge of God and assurance of salvation?

The four friends in the story were motivated by their friend's burden to the point that they did not care that it *had not been done this way before*. They broke the roof, the rules and the traditions all in one go! They were willing to break all of these to get their friend to Jesus. What about us? Are we willing to do things differently because we are more concerned about a hurting and lost generation than we are about keeping the status quo and upsetting a few traditionalists?

The four friends had to overcome *obstacles*

The four men arrived at the house at which Jesus was speaking and hit a problem: there was no way in because of the crowds. Many would have turned back at this point, but they put their heads together to overcome the obstacles.

There are, no doubt, many obstacles in the way of bringing our generation to Jesus. Some will be as old as the gospel itself; others will be unique features of the times in which we live. Many leaders talk to me about the obstacle of *apathy* – the sense that people just do not care about the message of Christianity and find it totally irrelevant to their lives. We could add that *syncretism* ('all roads lead to God') and *relativism* ('that's true for you but not for me') are other hallmarks of our post-modern age.

It is true that we face challenges, but I often think that many of today's Christians give up at the first hurdle. Not the men in the story – they found ways around the obstacle.

The four friends were *creative* and *innovative*

When they realized that the *usual* way to enter the house (i.e. the door!) was not going to work, they changed their approach. The way they entered was every bit as creative as it was innovative!

A friend of mine often says, 'If you're always doing what you've always done, then you will always have what you've always had.' Why do churches continue with well-worn approaches that are simply not working? We need a fresh approach to mission that says, 'If you can't go through the front door, then you might have to go through the roof!' In the story, we see that the men lowered their friend to Jesus through the roof. This was innovative, outside-the-box, creative thinking!

To achieve success in bringing people to Jesus, we need to do evangelism using new and creative ideas. To do things that have never been done before, it is no use looking to the past. John Wesley (1703–91) was an amazing evangelist but he was not an evangelist at the beginning of the third millennium. We must take the roof off our thinking. We need to (in the words of Captain Kirk) explore strange new worlds, seek out new life.

For starters – why are so many of us so reluctant to leave our church buildings and engage in genuine outreach? Some churches should re-name it 'in-draw' since their evangelism doesn't reach out at all.

What really is the most appropriate venue for our evangelistic event? It is probably not the church. Jesus told us that the church is to *go* into the entire world, not that the seekers were to *come* to our evening service. What about the pub, theatre, football stadium, coffee house, community centre . . .? Think large events, think small events, think community, think small groups – just think . . . and think outside the box. What about poets, DJs, the Internet, comedians, dancers, singers, storytellers? Think colourful, think community, think service, think incarnational, think spiritual – let us take the roof off our thinking.

I have come to understand two things about when we seek to do pioneer evangelism *outside the box*:

1. *Your actions invite criticism*

I always imagine that, as the four men lowered their friend to Jesus, there would have been people muttering disapprovingly in the corner. When I first did my evangelistic one-man comedy show, I was naturally apprehensive as to how it would turn out. One of my friends came to see it and, talking to me at the end, he strongly advised me to *never* do it again and to stick to preaching in churches. Sadly, you will always get some negative feedback from those who cannot see what you see. They want the safe and comfortable, and they do not like you doing something risky and unconventional.

My advice is to have a godly but visionary mentor, a trusted advisor who has your best interests at heart. This needs to be someone you listen to but someone who will bless you and allow you to go with your creative convictions as long as they are not heretical. If I had listened to that young friend on the first night of my show, I would never have seen theatres full of people who never normally go near a church, many of whom have responded to the story of the cross.

2. *Practise makes perfect*

When you try something new and creative, it is never perfect the first time. The nature of pioneer evangelism is that there are no well-worn paths – by definition people have not been this way before. This makes it exciting as well as a little daunting. Expect to make mistakes. Recognize that new ideas evolve. Be open to constructive criticism from others as to how you can improve what you're doing.

My show now looks very different to that first attempt and I want to keep on honing it and developing it to maximize its potential.

The four friends demonstrated *teamwork*

Fourthly, I love the element of teamwork we see in the story. The four men worked *together* to bring their friend to Jesus. As we consider doing pioneer evangelism through creative ideas, we need to recognize that no one person can do it alone. The age of the Lone Ranger is as dead as Tonto. We need to consider all the gifts and the strengths that the body of Christ has to offer, not just relying on the preacher, but incorporating the strengths of the many (the artist, the entrepreneur, the sportsman, the musician, the AV expert – to name but a few).

When we consider how incredibly diverse our culture is, it is becoming obvious that one size does *not* fit all. Therefore, we are going to need to utilize every part of the church and to engage in working together, if we are to bring this generation to Jesus.

If any of the four friends in the story had pulled out of the operation, it could have hindered the whole mission. Each friend had to play his part and carry his load. As evangelists, we need to involve some parts of the church that have been reluctant to get involved in evangelism. We need to fulfil our Ephesians 4:11 mandate as evangelists to 'equip the saints' by mobilizing the whole body, because the magnitude of the task requires that their gifting and strengths should be employed.

The four friends knew *they* weren't the answer!

Finally, the four friends were the embodiment of the maxim 'Let Jesus do what only Jesus can do.' Only Jesus can forgive sins. Only Jesus can heal. They knew they couldn't help their friend – but they knew a man who could.

Only Jesus can turn this generation around. One of the most exciting aspects of doing my evangelistic one-man show is witnessing the impact that the story of the cross has on people's lives.

The gospel message never changes, but our gospel methodology should never stay the same. It should change as long as culture changes. However good our innovative ideas seem, we must remember not to put our trust in our new methodology. When you have a fresh idea that proves effective, there is always a danger that you will shift subtly from relying on God, to relying on the new methodology. As success turns the criticism of men into the praise of men, it is easy for pride to take hold. I remember God speaking to me clearly, after I believed so strongly that my new idea was out of this world and could not fail. God drew my attention to Psalm 20:7 – 'Some trust in chariots and some in horses, but we trust in the name of the LORD our God' (NIV).

It is inevitable for pioneer evangelists that sometimes our new ideas will fail, but we must remember that God never fails us, and this is something to hold fast to when we are taking risks and stepping out of our comfort zone. The four friends in the story knew they had done their part – the rest was up to Jesus. It is only Christ who can reveal himself to people's hearts.

The mission of the four friends was to bring their friend to Jesus. Let us follow their example by saying to a world full of sickness and shame, 'I can't forgive you, I can't heal you – but I know a man who can!'

Chapter 14

Breaking Out from the Four Walls of the Church

Evangelism in the open air

Steve Legg

> We need to break out of our ecclesiastical ghettos and permeate non-Christian society.
>
> *The Lausanne Covenant*[1]

There I was, minding my own business, while out shopping one Saturday afternoon. Out of the corner of my eye I noticed an earnest-looking chap shouting about the Bible. He had a line of six 'brothers' behind him, looking equally earnest and all clutching big black Bibles.

Behind them stood the 'sisters' in their headscarves and overcoats. I stood for a while and watched and listened to the doom and gloom they were communicating. After they had finished their 'presentation' (to which, I might add, no one was paying a blind bit of notice), I just had to go and say something.

I explained that I was a Christian from a local church, and that I had a little experience when it came to presenting the good news in the open air. I thought I was pretty diplomatic, actually, as I attempted to make some subtle suggestions in terms of presentation, and how we should try to communicate fun and life in our message, and the importance of understanding crowd dynamics.

The preacher then asked where it talked about 'crowd dynamics' in the 'Word'. I thought it would be a good time to inject some humour to try to defuse the situation. And so I replied that, of course, the Bible doesn't mention crowd dynamics, but neither does it mention Jesus going to the toilet – but he obviously did!

The gentleman turned back to me, looked at my colourful Swatch wristwatch in disgust and declared in a loud voice, 'Well, you can't be a real Christian, anyway, wearing a watch like that!' And with that they all stormed off home. I couldn't believe it. Certainly not very good news – and anyway, what makes a Sekonda more spiritual than a Swatch?

Jesus did most of his ministry in the open air and in other places where large groups of men, women, boys and girls would gather. Take, for example, the conversation he had with a Samaritan woman (John 4:1–26). It's a wonderful example of Jesus ministering in the open air, going out of his way, smashing through cultural and religious barriers where everyone could see him, proclaiming the good news to a woman who was in great need and outside of respectable mainstream Judaism. We see in this example the real genius of open-air ministry: *When we minister outside we reach the outsider*. It seems such an obvious point to make, and yet nearly all of the church's evangelism is conducted inside religious buildings. Not surprisingly, we find ourselves more often than not preaching to the choir!

As we look through the Bible, we can see that neither Jesus nor his disciples relied solely on one-to-one evangelism. They often addressed larger crowds and most of the time these crowds were in the open air. On the Day of Pentecost, Peter stood up, full of the Holy Spirit, and 3,000 were saved in one go (Acts 2:14–41). Just imagine how long that would have taken if he'd used the one-to-one approach.

Breaking out from the four walls

Many others over the years have used open-air preaching to great effect. In the middle of the eighteenth century, preachers like George Whitefield and John Wesley were awesome outdoor preachers. Their preferred locations were town squares, but often the huge crowds that turned up made it necessary to preach in fields on the outskirts of town.

The religious establishment of the Church of England facilitated this by banning both these men from preaching in their churches – even though both were ordained ministers of that denomination. This did not deter them. Whitefield, followed by Wesley, took his message outside the four walls of the church – and many thousands were converted whom the church of the day had failed to reach.

What started negatively was clearly in God's sovereign plan. No wonder Wesley was later to state, 'The whole world is my parish.' One afternoon in Bristol, Whitefield preached in the open air on Kingswood Common to a crowd of 10,000 coalminers, whom Wesley described as 'England's worst specimens of humanity'. Whitefield's audience kept coming back for more.

Even in his eighty-eighth year Wesley kept preaching outdoors. On 7 October 1790 he preached for the last time in the open air, under an ash tree in Winchelsea. Arranging the meeting for noon, so everyone who worked could attend in their lunchtime, he preached his last ever sermon: 'The Kingdom of heaven is at hand; repent ye, and believe the Gospel'. Under that ash tree, known today as the Wesley Tree, 'the Word was with mighty power and the tears of the people flowed in torrents.'

I love open-air work. There is nothing like going onto the streets and proclaiming the gospel. I have personally seen hundreds become Christians through open-air ministry. There are many other benefits as well:

- You will raise the profile of Jesus: 'But I, when I am lifted up from the earth, will draw all [people] to myself' (John 12:32 NIV). The Greek verb *hupsoo*, 'lifted up', is used literally but also metaphorically, in the sense of exalting the name of Jesus. This is what we do when we lift his name up on the streets, and it has tremendous power.
- You are able to reach people who aren't Christians. If they don't come to us, then we should go to them. You can reach large numbers very effectively – it really is not unusual to reach several hundred during a two-hour open-air session.
- It will significantly raise the profile of your church. Your church should be part of your community, so let your community know about you. This is often much harder for some of the 'new' churches that don't have a permanent building or specific place of worship. Going onto the streets will let people know that you are there for them.
- You will smash misconceptions about Christians being boring and miserable, by demonstrating fun, friendship and life: 'I have come that they may have life, and have it to the full' (John 10:10 NIV). Go and demonstrate the abundant life that you have received,

so others might find it so attractive that they'll want it too.
- Working on the streets will build faith in you and give you and your team the opportunity to pray for people, perform and preach – maybe for the first time.

I'm sure you can think of many other benefits of doing open-air work. There are many different ways of doing it. Once again, what follows isn't a comprehensive guide, but ideas and thoughts to whet your appetite. Here are some of the things I have been involved with over the years and which I know work.

Detached street evangelism

This is the most simple form of open-air evangelism. You simply find out where people are and go out in pairs and chat to them, building friendships and showing care and concern that will practically demonstrate the love of God. There are six things to bear in mind when undertaking detached work.

1. Be prepared

Before you and your mission partner go out for the first time, conduct a quick reconnaissance trip to see who is out and about, and more importantly where they are. Perhaps during the week, your local young people hang about outside the local chip shop. They're there every evening from around 7 p.m. until 10 p.m. Just imagine the kind of impact you could have on those young lives, meeting with them on a consistent basis. You could, after all, be the only example of a real Christian they'll ever get to meet.

2. Be friends

Relax and enjoy your times out on the streets. Of course it will be daunting going out for the first time and striking up a conversation with a complete stranger, but it is such an effective way of reaching people who wouldn't necessarily come near a church. So relax – take a chill pill! Your primary aim is not to evangelize but to have fun making new friends and, as a by-product of that, to sow seeds of hope and truth. People are nearly always up for talking and they respond well to genuine friendliness. Believe that you'll see the fruit of all this sowing time.

3. Be committed

Commitment is of utmost importance – especially since many of the young people you encounter will have been let down in the past by authority figures in their lives. Friendships take time, so when you have a particularly good contact, follow it up by agreeing to meet again. Successful detached work demands a regular commitment. Perhaps the young people you are working with are really into skating, for example. Now you might not have ever been on a skateboard or roller-blades in your life (or the last time you did, they were called roller-skates!). Don't feel that to reach this group you need to rush out and buy all the gear and equipment so you can be part of their gang too. You'd probably look very silly and it could easily end up being counter-productive. You need to be authentically *you*, and if you are older than the kids, don't try to be one of them. They probably don't need mates but one thing many young people do need is a safe older parent/older sibling figure whom they can respect and come to for advice.

4. Be of service

Discover ways you can make a difference in their lives. Suppose the group has always had hassle from local people who object to their skating around their streets – you could see how you could help them really practically. Perhaps you could work with the council in trying to find them a place to skate, or get some money together to build some ramps, or whatever. They'll soon start to ask why you're doing it. Having someone to fight their corner is a sure-fire way to earn their respect.

5. Be sensible

There is great strength in going in pairs, and it makes approaching a large group a little easier. However, two people approaching a single person could appear threatening, so be flexible and sensitive on this one. For obvious reasons it's not ideal for a lad to chat to a girl one-on-one, or the other way around. Your intentions may be perfectly pure and godly, but the person you're talking to may not have quite the same perception or intentions. Equally, it's not a good idea for a couple of girls to approach a large group of lads and vice versa, so I favour having a male and female in each team. Mixed teams really help to avoid unnecessary confusion!

6. Be open to God

Approaching complete strangers and talking to them could be the ideal moment for you to use spiritual gifts – such as prophecy. Ask God to reveal things about the people you're conversing with. That's what Jesus did in his encounter with the woman at the well (John 4:1–26,39–41), and it had a major effect.

Praise and worship

Praise and worship have always played a significant part in revivals through history and, throughout the Bible, praise and worship is linked to the context of warfare. We can read one such instance in the Old Testament when Judah was confronted by her mortal enemies Moab and Ammon. Jehoshaphat sent musicians out in front of his army, and the result of the praise and worship was victory:

> After consulting the people, Jehoshaphat appointed men to sing to the LORD and to praise him for the splendour of his holiness as they went out at the head of the army, saying:
>
> 'Give thanks to the LORD, for his love endures for ever.'
>
> As they began to sing and praise, the LORD set ambushes against the men of Ammon and Moab and Mount Seir who were invading Judah, and they were defeated.
>
> 2 Chronicles 20:21–22 NIV

When we worship in our streets, precincts and parks we engage in spiritual warfare – declaring to the principalities and powers that their 'rule' is temporary and that Christ is the true King who will one day establish his kingdom in fullness on the earth.

Music is less confrontational than preaching and, done well, it can attract a crowd who find it intriguing and disarming. As you step out to do this, it will build faith in you and your team and, as we've noted already, when we lift Jesus up (John 12:32), he will draw all men, women, boys and girls to himself. It will also give you an opportunity to discover something of God's heart and compassion for the area you're in and the people who live and work there, and to turn this into intercession.

Surveys and questionnaires

Once again, these are really tools to get you chatting to people, which could well steer you onto a conversation about Jesus.

In the past I've often used one question on a large board set up in the middle of a precinct. Something daft like: 'Do you believe in the Loch Ness Monster?' I've kept score of people's responses, and it's not unusual for passers-by to stop their shopping and come over to offer their opinion. As I've just said, it's another tool to steer you onto asking about more important views, opinions and beliefs.

If you're using a survey or questionnaire, then have it properly printed and secure it onto a clipboard. Work in pairs and take it in turns to ask the question. Have a small gift, maybe a good-quality, glossy Gospel (which of course has been pre-printed with your church's contact details and service times on the back), for everyone who takes the time and trouble to be surveyed.

Literature

This could either be invitational or an explanation of the gospel. The first could be an invitation to a special guest event at your church (Alpha supper, carol service, guest speaker, etc.), or a brochure advertising your church and its services. Don't forget the date, time of start *and* finish, location (perhaps with a map), price (if applicable), contact phone number and email address, and a brief description of the event(s).

The second form of literature would be an accessible explanation of the gospel. It could be a personal story tract (more about this later) or a simple, well-illustrated and well-produced gospel explanation.

Drama

Good drama is an excellent form of communication. It will appeal to all ages and backgrounds and can draw and hold huge crowds. I certainly don't claim to be an expert thespian, but from years of experience I can offer a few tips:

1. *Keep it polished*

Performances on the street are a shop window of what church and Christianity are all about. You are not going for an Oscar, but strive for excellence and make your sketches as polished and professional as possible.

2. *Keep it real*

Demonstrate energy, fun and life, and show what Christianity is *really* like, smashing loads of misconceptions in the process.

3. *Keep it short*

Make your drama short, sweet and to the point! Perhaps focus on the effects of sin, or Jesus' work on the cross. Don't make it an epic of *Ben Hur* proportions – some passers-by will only linger for a few minutes. Remember KISS – Keep It Short and Sweet!

4. Keep it visual

If you don't have a PA system, which you probably won't on the majority of occasions, you don't want the crowd to miss your point because they can't hear the words. Keep the dialogue to an absolute minimum and use props and gestures that are easily understood.

5. Keep it memorable

Good drama, well done, will stick in people's minds. It's true that a picture is worth a thousand words, so leave good, fun, positive pictures with your audience.

Preaching

When you preach in the open air, you only have a few minutes to share your message, so think clearly what you're going to say and what you're not going to say. Keep it simple and straightforward and make just *one* clear point.

Be as natural as you can be and build a rapport with your listeners; after all, communication isn't just *what* you say, it's *how* you say it. Your appearance, attitude and demeanour speak volumes too. Be gracious and take any heckling in a good-humoured way (it might happen!). Remember, you are called not just to *preach* good news but to *be* good news!

Presentation

This is a mix of probably all of the above and is what I personally enjoy doing best, because it's so much fun and changes lives in the process. The programme will be short – fifteen to twenty minutes absolute maximum – and will be fast-moving, humorous, will grab attention and have the gospel message threaded throughout. Because the crowd will change, you should run the programme a few times, and use the time in between for conversations. A good programme might run like this:

- Praise and worship: 5 minutes.
- Introduction: 1 minute.
- Drama: 3 minutes.
- Testimony: 2 minutes.
- Drama: 3 minutes.
- Preach: 2 minutes.

Don't forget . . .

- The praise and worship at the beginning of the programme isn't there necessarily to draw a crowd, though invariably it will. Instead, it is for the team to focus on God, to build faith and to invite God's presence to come in power on the streets.
- At the end of the worship, your team becomes rent-a-crowd and forms a nice loose semicircle that looks in at your compère, who welcomes the crowd and looks after proceedings.
- Talk to people whenever you can – it's much better than just handing out leaflets.
- Take plenty of mints with you for those who may have enjoyed a curry or a loaf of garlic bread the night before!
- Put one person in charge of all props, their delivery, return and safe-keeping during the time on the streets. Similarly, have someone else in charge of all publicity materials, tracts, Gospels, questionnaires,

clipboards, pens and anything else you might need.
- Don't give out literature or interrupt people while they're still watching the presentation.
- At the end of the preaching your team *immediately* gets into conversations with the audience and asks them what they thought of the presentation.
- Smile and enjoy it.
- Pray for and expect people to become Christians.

Concluding appendices

1. The law

It is our constitutional right, under English common law, to present the gospel on the streets. We are guaranteed freedom of speech and assembly in public places, which of course includes most streets, roads, pavements, parks and most shopping centres. I use the word 'most' because over the years, many local councils have introduced bylaws to limit what happens on the streets. Also, some privately owned shopping centres will not allow you access.

The major problem I have encountered is that of obstruction, so the choice of your venue is an important factor. You might be moved on if you cause an obstruction. In practice, I have found that the police very rarely take any action unless the blockage you and your audience are causing is fairly major.

You will normally need permission to use a PA system, but even if this is granted you need to be sensitive that you are not 'disturbing the peace', otherwise once again you could be asked to stop. With training and practice you will be able to learn how to project your voice without the help of a PA. Indeed, I was once moved on for disturbing the peace in Leicester Square in Central London, and that was without a microphone and amplifier!

Finally, on the subject of the law, if you have obtained written permission for your open-air event, then make sure you have it with you, just in case of any problems.

2. *Hecklers*

Because of my humorous, interactive style I'm often getting heckled and I have to admit, most of the time I really enjoy it. There was one time, however, at a large event at Plymouth University, when it started to get on my nerves. For my full 45-minute performance one lad interrupted and heckled me continually. I carried on undaunted, using my best and most rehearsed ad-libs (that's a contradiction if ever I heard one!) and presented the gospel message to the best of my ability. I came offstage to find this very same lad sat at my table, grinning from ear to ear, having bought me a pint of lager. 'You were great,' he said. 'I heckle everyone and you did a great job. It didn't faze you one bit, did it?' I took all this as a compliment, though for one fleeting moment I couldn't decide whether to drink the pint or tip it over his head – in love, of course!

I have found from experience that most hecklers fall into two categories: humorous or drunk. They are almost always good-natured, though, and you can use their interaction to great effect. It's well worth practising, rehearsing and filing at the back of your mind a selection of nice humorous retorts to hecklers. You and I know we have prepared them in advance, but your audience will think you're incredibly quick-witted and will listen to what else you have to say! A few of my favourite put-down lines are:

- He's a legend in his own lunchtime.
- Are you a figment of your own imagination?
- I've heard a lot about you. Now I'd like to hear your side.
- Please save all the questions until I leave.
- I'll provide the dialogue.
- I don't bother you when you're working.
- Hey, you're the guy who heckled me ten years ago. I never forget a suit.
- I'm sorry, I couldn't hear you. I was talking.
- Did your brains come with instructions?
- Sir, you have a ready wit. Let me know when it's ready.

Well, I hope all of that helps. The streets and precincts of our nation contain fertile ground, so let's get out there and sow some gospel seed, and believe God that it will produce a harvest. Jesus always believed God for great things: 'Everything is possible for him who believes' (Mark 9:23 NIV). The early church was certainly up for it, so let's follow their example. Let's leave the comfort zone of the four walls of the church and go and make a difference in the open air!

Chapter 15

Out of Africa
Evangelism in a cross-cultural context

Ian Wilson

> A missionary is not someone who crosses the sea but is someone who has seen the cross.
>
> J.John

Re-thinking mission

After three and a half hours on a pot-holed Tanzanian road in a truck that had never possessed a shock-absorber in its life, we arrived at the orphanage to meet the 'missionary sisters'. During the long journey my imagination had gone into overdrive as to what these 'missionary sisters' would be like: 100 years old, hair in a bun, jam-jar glasses, and buck teeth? Thankfully, they were nothing like my appalling stereotype, and I married Sister Andie eighteen months later!

As I write this, years later, I now live in Tanzania, in a city called Mwanza. It has a population of about 700,000 people and sits on the edge of Lake Victoria. It is the principal city of a region of about 13 million people spread across eleven districts.

To some I am 'the missionary', but for me I am simply a bloke who loves Jesus and wants to take those risky steps of faith in following him and make a difference to people's lives. My mate J.John says, 'A missionary is not someone who crosses the sea but is someone who sees the cross.'

Seeing the cross, for us as a family, has brought us to Tanzania, but we are still *ordinary* people allowing our *extraordinary* God to use us to make a difference in the lives we seek to touch on a daily basis here. For *you* it may involve your work colleagues, neighbours, your town or village – where you are *now*!

This chapter is subtitled 'Evangelism in a cross-cultural context' because, in the multi-cultural society in which we live, cross-cultural mission can occur on our doorstep and need not require travelling to another part of the world.

Defining authentic mission

> Incarnation (*Latin*): 1. The act of clothing with flesh, or becoming embodied in flesh. 2. (*Theol.*) The union of the second person of the Godhead with manhood in Christ.[1]

The incarnation is one of the central tenets of Christianity: God becomes a human being in the person of Jesus Christ. To put it another way, Jesus is 'God with skin on'.

Greg Downes states: 'All authentic mission is by definition incarnational: it bears the three hallmarks of being contextual, relational and sacrificial.' Let's consider the elements of what it means to do evangelism in a cross-cultural context under these three headings.

Incarnational mission is *contextual*

That is to say, it takes place in a real-life situation. This could be a place or a people group that your work brings you into contact with. It does not happen in a vacuum. For me, that context is the job I do (being a dentist) and the place I live (Tanzania). I am a dentist *and* an evangelist – a unique combination if ever there was one. 'This won't hurt a bit, sir . . . especially if you give your life to Jesus *now*!'

Andie and I lead an NGO called Bridge2aid (www.bridge2aid.org). The ethos is simple: the dental centre we have opened generates capital to train Tanzanian primary health-care workers to take out teeth safely in remote areas. We also fund the provision of food, medical care and clothing to the poor and homeless communities of the city. These *Maskini* are the untouchables of Tanzanian society – suffering with HIV or leprosy or disabilities, they have had their dignity, self-worth and creativity stripped from them. We are ordinary people who have *seen the cross* and the difference that an extraordinary God can make with us and through us for the benefit of others.

1. Contextual mission means invading the culture

This will vary hugely from context to context. What thing do I need to do so I can get under the skin of the culture I am called to reach? Where there is a different tongue, this will involve learning the language. For us in Tanzania, this was unavoidable if we were to penetrate the culture effectively.

Now learning a new language is, to me, about as inspiring as 'pulling teeth' for you! (Apologies, but being a dentist, I had to get this in somewhere!) Not being able to communicate leads to all sorts of frustrations and adds to the feeling of culture shock, disorientation and isolation – hardly the conditions in which to reach people! I had already taken some lessons when we first arrived, but my progress was slow, much to the disgust of my naturally linguistic wife. Every Tuesday evening, Andie would frown at my attempts and the teacher, Mama George, would laugh . . . so at least someone was happy. I'm sure Mama George put up with me for so long just for the comedy value.

My noble attempts to speak the language included the following: Instead of telling my patients to 'wait outside the surgery in reception', I was telling them to 'quietly tiptoe out the room and sit in a corner'. The best by far was when I was visiting a remote village, and I went up to two women. Instead of asking for 'two cups of cold drinking water for my children', I apparently said, 'Please can I have two cups of cold urine for my children – they are very thirsty.'

But I persisted, as I wanted to invade the culture for Christ!

2. Contextual mission means being sensitive to the culture

One of my first experiences of the differences in culture here in Tanzania involved an innocent bottle of Coke. I had just finished preaching in the morning service and my throat felt like a dry gravel path. We all went to the pastor's house, sat down, placed our order for drinks, and started to relax and chat. A few minutes later the ice-cold drinks arrived – my tongue was almost losing the will to live now – so as soon as the bottle was opened and passed to me, I said, 'Down the hatch – thank you, Jesus!'

However, after the second glug I felt the swift blow of Andie's sandal on my shin (which usually means I've erred in some way), and several pairs of eyes gazing at me. The pastor looked at me as he said, 'Shall we pray before we enjoy God's provision?' Now don't laugh, because you would have done the same! In a wonderful but different way to me, my African brothers and sisters would literally thank God for everything before they enjoyed it. I needed to become culturally sensitive to this.

On a more serious note, one of the things that causes me frustration is the ability of the church to put unnecessary *barriers* in the way of people coming to Christ. For example, here in Mwanza 30 per cent of the population are Muslims, yet the church has its 'crusade season' (obviously without thinking through the historical significance of the Crusades, which were launched in 1095 to liberate Jerusalem from Muslim rule). During this season, platforms are built and PA systems are set up to carry the sound of evangelists growling the saving message of Jesus until the early hours of the morning.

We need to be sensitive to the culture we are called to, so that we are not needlessly offensive and do not create unnecessary barriers to people coming to faith.

Incarnational mission is *relational*

That is to say, it is people-centred. It is primarily not about projects or methodology or even eloquent preaching, but about people.

1. Relational mission loves people

It is amazing how often the church passionately proclaims that God loves people but communicates something quite different.

A while back, when we were still living in the UK, a few of the church lads had started to meet up with the non-church bunch for no other reason than to enjoy their friendship, have a couple of drinks and have a laugh. I asked the wife of one of the church guys if he had enjoyed himself.

'Oh yes,' she said, 'he had a great time.'

'Fantastic,' I said. 'Let's get more of the church lads there next week, then.'

Her reply left me not only annoyed but saddened that even today this attitude still existed in the church. 'Oh, I don't think we could get more of the church lads going. After all, there was a bar and people were drinking alcohol. And some in the church think we shouldn't mix with those sorts!'

Amazing isn't it? Jesus, the friend of sinners, loves us, dies for us, calls us his friends – and then we get so *religious* that we fail to engage with the 'sort' he wants us to befriend in his name. If he was a friend of sinners, then I should be too, even if it offends the religious culture that surrounds me.

Another example of mis-communicating to non-Christians can be our refusal to allow them to serve on teams alongside Christians – I am sticking my neck out here. In Tanzania we have the privilege of many volunteers coming to visit us every year to get involved in our community outreach projects. I believe that while many Christian missions have the policy of taking Christians only, this can easily communicate that we (and therefore our faith) are exclusive. We accept non-Christian volunteers as well, and many are impacted by what they experience and some come to faith.

2. Relational mission is holistic

Vinay Samuel and Chris Sugden write in *Mission as Transformation: A Theology of the Whole Gospel*:

> Holistic evangelism means that we take the situation in which people are – the situation which bothers them, which constantly affects their lives – and show how the Gospel and Jesus are relevant in and to their situation.[2]

Much mission talk today revolves around such jargon terms as 'the 10/40 window', 'the adopt-a-people movement' and 'unreached peoples'. In his grace God has used such expressions to motivate people to more active involvement in evangelistic church-planting mission in some of the neediest parts of the world. But in the Book of Acts, we see that mission is a much bigger calling than just church-planting evangelism. Paul also engaged in a long-term teaching ministry (e.g. Acts 19:9–10; 20:31). He returned to churches he had planted in order to encourage and strengthen the Christians there. In Acts 20 he ministers to the elders of the church in Ephesus. In the 'Great Commission' of Matthew 28 we see that mission involves teaching people to obey everything the Lord has commanded us. And in Luke's Gospel we see that the task of mission includes not only preaching and teaching, but also social ministries for the poor and oppressed (Luke 4:18–19). So Luke has a holistic picture of the task of witness and mission – so should we.

3. Relational mission is empowering

> Again Jesus said, 'Peace be with you! As the Father has sent me, I am sending you.' And with that he breathed on them and said, 'Receive the Holy Spirit. If you forgive anyone his sins, they are forgiven; if you do not forgive them, they are not forgiven.'
>
> John 20:21–23 NIV

Jesus' form of mission was not just relational; he *empowered* people to engage in mission themselves. In my context, for the white man to come in with his mega-bucks and tell people what to do is not helpful and smacks of the days of colonial rule. We need to empower people to do the stuff themselves.

This is a principle for all mission, whatever the context. Our role is to teach people to fish rather than doing it for them or buying a big fishing boat without the training to go with it!

Incarnational mission is *sacrificial*

That is to say, it is costly. The incarnation involved sacrifice on Christ's part, as we are reminded in Philippians 2:7–8:

> [He] made himself nothing, taking the very nature of a servant, being made in human likeness. And being found in appearance as a man, he humbled himself and became obedient to death – even death on a cross! (NIV)

1. Sacrificial mission may entail financial hardship

One of the main challenges of cross-cultural overseas work is how to finance the grassroots, day-to-day operations. Traditionally, missionaries have been dependent on their sending churches, often in the developed world. As the growth of Christianity has shifted to developing nations, this model looks increasingly colonial and anachronistic, and I question whether it is the right one.

In Corinth, Paul stayed in the home of Aquila and Priscilla, who were tent-makers by profession. Although such work was despised because it dealt with the skins of dead animals, it seems that somehow Paul had also learned this skill, and so he worked with them while seeking to evangelize in the city. It would seem that Paul earned his living by his own hands when there was as yet no local church to support him. But we also know that when he had planted a living church in Macedonia, they supported him financially (Phil. 4:10ff). This is the model I use working as a dentist in my culture.

Is this a useful model for modern mission? Should cross-cultural overseas mission workers support *themselves* when working in places where there is no local church? Should missionaries *normally* be supported by the receiving churches rather than by their home sending churches? This model may not give financial security and may even involve financial hardship, but it does empower the indigenous churches and is an amazing way for the missionary to get under the skin of the local culture.

2. *Sacrificial mission will entail suffering*

Not a popular message, but a biblical one!

A while ago I asked my kids the question, 'What do you do if you see a snake?' Jake, who is a mature grown man in a four-year-old's body, repeated the answer I had relentlessly drilled into him: 'I run away as fast as I can and go straight to Mummy and Daddy.' Imani, my three-year-old daughter, had a rather different answer to my question: 'Oh Daddy, if I see a snake I will talk to it, pick it up and bring it home!' I had failed!

My snake-defence lessons were quickly forgotten until one evening, when both kids were in the bath and I lay snoozing on the couch. Suddenly the high-pitched scream of 'Daddy! *Snake*!' came from the bathroom.

Images of a 35-foot cobra flashed through my head as I got armed to the teeth with everything and anything.

What good the TV remote would have been I don't know, but it seemed a good idea at the time. I ran into the bathroom, ready to meet the monster! Dad to the rescue! Jake and Imani, both now fairly hysterical, pointed to the uninvited snake. What was it? A cobra or a black mamba ready to strike? None of the above! Our snake was a poor five-inch 'worm' that was desperately fleeing to the safety of the plug-hole from the two big monsters who were making a huge amount of noise and had disturbed its kip! Casually (with a heart rate still of 455) I picked up our 'snake' and helped him to safety – my every move watched by four wide eyes, two gawping mouths and several drools of saliva! That's right – I am Ian the Snake Catcher! A hero? Oh yes – to my kids.

The type of suffering resulting from sacrificial mission will depend on the call. For those, like me, called to live in a different culture, it may take the form of *culture shock*. For many people, when we talk about crossing cultures by going overseas, the first thing to crop up is how we will cope with the dreaded culture shock. This is a term used to describe the anxiety and feelings (of surprise, disorientation, confusion etc.) that people experience when they have to operate within an entirely different cultural or social environment, such as a foreign country. It grows out of the difficulties in assimilating the new culture, such as knowing what is appropriate and what is not. This is often combined with a certain disgust (moral or aesthetic) about some aspects of the new or different culture.

Severe culture shock (moving to a foreign country) often consists of distinct phases. Not everyone moves through the phases and not everyone is in the new culture long enough to pass through all three:

(a) The honeymoon phase

During this period, the differences between the old and new cultures are seen in a romantic light – everything is wonderful and new. For example, in moving to a new country, you might love the new foods, the pace of life, the people's habits, the buildings and so on.

(b) The negotiation phase

After a few days, a few weeks or a few months, minor differences between the old and new cultures are resolved. You may long for food the way it is prepared 'back home', you may find the pace of life too fast or slow, or you may find the people's habits annoying.

One example of this cultural negotiation came when we were looking around a Tanzanian's house, considering renting it as our home. On entering the household of this very religious family, we were greeted by every piece of Christian kitsch you could imagine. Of particular interest was a hologram of Jesus in the corner. As you approached it you saw Jesus dead on the cross, but as you continued to move, suddenly Jesus opened his eyes and was alive! The resurrection symbolism was lost as, if you moved slightly, he died again. Now would you rent that house? Yep, we did! But the Jesus hologram *didn't stay*!

(c) The 'everything is OK' phase

After a while (weeks or months) you grow accustomed to the new culture's differences and develop routines. At this point, you no longer react to the new culture positively or negatively, because it no longer feels like a 'new' culture. You become concerned with basic living again, as you were in your home culture.

In some severe cases, it may be impossible to deal with culture shock. Some people give up trying to assimilate into the new culture and return home.

Another example of sacrifice in the context of overseas cross-cultural mission is in the family and friendships you leave behind. This is the tough one. There is the re-negotiation of relationships because they all exist at a different level now. Where once you met down the pub, you now meet online; where once you had meals together most months, you now do so once a year if you are fortunate enough to come back to home base annually, as we do. Some of my North American missionary friends can only go back to the USA every four years!

I remember battling the confusion of leaving my elderly parents when I came to live in East Africa, especially as I was their only child. It might help if I make it personal: a few years ago I travelled back to the UK to be with Andie and the kids, as our third child was due to be born. The skies above Heathrow welcomed me with a beautiful sunny morning and even the British Airways ground staff seemed to have collectively swallowed 'happy to help' pills that day. I was to fly straight up to Newcastle and then go to see Dad, who had been in several nursing homes since suffering a stroke in 2003 and Mum's death in November 2004. Dad – Basil Charles Wilson – just wanted 'to go home to be with Jesus and be at peace', and every time I had seen him he had asked his missionary son, 'Can you put a good word in, Son, with Jesus to get my room in the mansion ready?' A man of quiet, personal faith, he was my hero, pouring himself out sacrificially for the life of his only (often unappreciative) son.

Once I had arrived at the nursing home, the Wilson family and friends sat around him and went into action. Laughing with him, cracking jokes and holding his hand. His physical limitations were evident but the life and character still shone through. Later, as we left after having several fun-filled hours together, I hugged him close and kissed him goodbye on the cheek. It was to be the last time I would ever do this.

The next morning, 'his room must have been ready', as Jesus took him home. Nursing staff later told me that Dad had been saying, 'I'll wait to see Ian and then I will go.' The fact that God allowed us to have those few hours together, after I had returned home from thousands of miles away, was a grace moment for me. On 12 June 2005 my Dad went 'home' and on 15 July 2005 our third child, Neema Grace Wilson, was born.

Authentic cross-cultural mission is costly but, as J.John says, 'The cause is worth the cost.'

Not every Christian is called to be a cross-cultural evangelist, let alone one overseas. Every Christian is called to be a global Christian, however. A global Christian is a follower of Jesus who is concerned with the mission of God wider than in their local context. He or she is a believer so captivated by the glory of God that they choose to align themselves with God's mission to fill the earth with the knowledge of the glory of God, as the waters cover the sea (Hab. 2:14)!

Chapter 16

God the Evangelist
Prayer in evangelism

Greg Downes

> The most important human factor in effective evangelism is prayer. Every great awakening in the history of the Church from the time of the apostles until today has been the result of prayer. There have been great awakenings without much preaching, and there have been great awakenings with absolutely no organization, but there has never been a true awakening without much prayer.
>
> R. A. Torrey (1856–1928)[1]

Occasionally I meet a Christian who is convinced that evangelism is *not* for them. Preaching isn't their gift, they don't believe in power evangelism, they are not sharp enough for apologetics – the list goes on.

I suggest that one enterprise that is part of evangelism they can *definitely* do is prayer.

Is praying for the lost biblical?

When I was a teenager, a clergyman commented to me that he questioned whether praying for the lost to come to Christ was a biblical practice. This had the undesired effect of sapping my enthusiasm for intercession for non-Christians – which was not great anyway.

While there is not a direct exhortation to pray for the lost to be saved, we can be confident that it is consistent with scriptural teaching. The apostle Paul wrote to Timothy:

> I urge, then, first of all, that requests, prayers, intercession and thanksgiving be made for everyone – for kings and all those in authority, that we may live peaceful and quiet lives in all godliness and holiness. This is good, and pleases God our Saviour, who wants all men to be saved and to come to a knowledge of the truth.
>
> 1 Timothy 2:1–4 NIV

In these words, Paul stresses the importance of prayer when the church meets together; in particular he exhorts prayer for the civil authorities and goes on to link it to both *peace* and *salvation*. Paul also prays that his own people group would come to salvation:

> Brothers, my heart's desire and prayer to God for the Israelites is that they may be saved.
>
> Romans 10:1 NIV

It is little surprise, then, that a global gathering of theologians at the International Consultation on the Relationship between Evangelism and Social Responsibility in 1982 pledged as follows:

> We resolve ourselves, and call upon our churches, to take much more seriously the period of intercession in public worship . . . to focus our prayers . . . on the evangelization of the world (closed lands, resistant peoples,

> missionaries, national churches). We long to see every Christian congregation bowing down in humble and expectant faith before our Sovereign Lord.[2]

The Lausanne Committee for World Evangelization met in Pattaya, Thailand in 2004. This gathering produced a paper entitled *Prayer in Evangelism*. The definition given for 'prayer in evangelism' was:

> Prayer for the unsaved, asking the Lord to draw them to Himself (John 6:44); to open their ears to understand the truth (Matthew 13:19); and to open their eyes to see the light of the gospel (2 Corinthians 4:4). It also involves praying for ourselves that we may have compassion for the spiritual well-being of unbelievers, and be open to sharing the good news as He opens the door of opportunity. Simply put, in evangelistic praying we talk to God about people and then talk to people about God.[3]

In this chapter we will look at a snapshot of life in the early church and see the intimate connection between prayer and evangelism under the headings, 'The primacy of prayer', 'The practice of prayer' and 'The power of prayer'. Acts 6:1–7 records:

> In those days when the number of disciples was increasing, the Grecian Jews among them complained against the Hebraic Jews because their widows were being overlooked in the daily distribution of food. So the Twelve gathered all the disciples together and said, 'It would not be right for us to neglect the ministry of the word of God in order to wait on tables. Brothers, choose seven men from among you who are known to be full of the Spirit and wisdom. We will turn this responsibility over to them and will give our attention to prayer and the ministry of the word.'

> This proposal pleased the whole group. They chose Stephen, a man full of faith and of the Holy Spirit; also Philip, Procorus, Nicanor, Timon, Parmenas, and Nicolas from Antioch, a convert to Judaism. They presented these men to the apostles, who prayed and laid their hands on them.
>
> So the word of God spread. The number of disciples in Jerusalem increased rapidly, and a large number of priests became obedient to the faith (NIV).

The primacy of prayer

> We will turn this responsibility over to them and will give our attention to prayer.

The early church knew about the primacy of prayer. The Twelve appointed deacons because they did not want to be distracted from their primary calling, which was to preach and to pray. The early church prayed as a first resource. We pray as a last resort.

Billy Graham wrote an article in *Christianity Today* entitled 'Recovering the Primacy of Evangelism'.[4] He wrote as the second millennium drew to a close:

> We are commanded to be faithful in proclaiming the Word – and yet, at the same time, every success, every advance, no matter how slight, is possible only because God has been at work by the Holy Spirit. The Spirit gives us the message, leads us to those he has prepared, and brings conviction of sin and new life.
>
> When we understand that truth, it frees us from the temptation to use manipulation or pressure. It also should free us from pride and boasting, because we know that God alone must receive the credit for whatever is accomplished.

> When we understand that truth, we also will realize the urgency of prayer in evangelism. My own ministry, I am convinced, has only been possible because of the countless men and women who have prayed. I never stand before an audience without sensing those prayers and sensing also my own dependence on God the Holy Spirit to accomplish his work. The words from Zechariah should be written indelibly on our hearts and minds: '"Not by might nor by power, but by my Spirit," says the LORD Almighty' (Zech. 4:6).

When we genuinely accept that God is the evangelist and salvation belongs to him alone, we will not just pray that he blesses our evangelism but pray before we ever undertake it. As John Wesley said, 'Everything by prayer and nothing without it.'

The practice of prayer

> They presented these men to the apostles, who prayed.

The early church knew about the practice of prayer. They did not have the plethora of books, guides and manuals on prayer that we have, but it was part of their life and mission. Despite all our resources, it is something we speak about more than we practise. 'Before God sends revival he begins to mobilize his people in prayer,' noted Matthew Henry (1662–1714).

R. A. Torrey fervently believed this – that no lasting evangelistic move of God was possible without the practice of prayer. He writes in his journal of personal experience of the Welsh revival:

> The great Welsh revival in 1904 and 1905 was unquestionably the outcome of prayer . . . at first the work went

> very slowly. There were great crowds, most enthusiastic singing, but little manifestation of real convicting and regenerating power. A day of fasting and prayer was appointed . . . there came an immediate turn of the tide; the power of God fell. On that day, at a meeting held in another part of Wales by a few devoted men of God, the power of God was manifested in a most remarkable way. The week following the meetings in Cardiff a minister associated with the work went up into one of the valleys of Wales, and there was a mighty manifestation of the power of God with large numbers of conversions, and all over Wales the work of God continued, largely without human instruments except in the way of prayer. 100,000 conversions were reported in a year . . . it was one of the most remarkable works of God in modern times, and from Wales there went forth a fire from God to the uttermost parts of the earth and only eternity will reveal the glorious results of that work.[5]

For many people the question that arises is: *How* do I go about the practice of praying for the lost? It is important that we employ a method that facilitates *focused* and *persistent* intercession. The key is not to pray for our non-Christian friends erratically and occasionally but rather to decide on a few and faithfully intercede for them until we see a spiritual breakthrough.

In considering a plan to pray for the lost, many have taken Acts 1:8 as a framework for intercession as well as mission:

> you will be my witnesses in Jerusalem, and in all Judea and Samaria, and to the ends of the earth (NIV).

It is interesting to note the pattern that Jesus established for mission. He said:

You will be my witnesses
in Jerusalem,
and in all Judea
and Samaria,
and to the ends of the earth.

To understand the picture that Jesus was painting, it is imperative to understand the geography. Jerusalem was the Jews' Holy City – the place of the Temple and the epicentre of their world. Judea was the province in which Jerusalem was located, and Samaria was the neighbouring province.

Jesus was getting his disciples to imagine concentric circles, reaching ever outward. First, the disciples were to be witnesses to the immediate community in which they found themselves – Jerusalem. Then they were to expand their mission to the region, then the adjoining region and, finally, they were to expand their ministry internationally. One way of using prayer in evangelism in a disciplined way that does not become too introspective and takes account of the bigger picture is to use this as a model.

Commit to having four *prayer circles* in a spiritual journal and pray for three people/situations in each sphere: your *Jerusalem* (your immediate family, friends and work colleagues); your *Judea* (your city, town or village); your *Samaria* (the nation); and *the ends of the earth* (the mission of God overseas – especially in lands closed or hostile to the gospel).

Ed Silvoso, in his helpful book *Prayer Evangelism*, comes up with some practical guidelines that develop the role of prayer in evangelism a step beyond simply intercession.[6] This is relevant in praying for people in your Jerusalem circle, in which, because of immediate relationship, intercession can be translated into action.

Silvoso looks at Luke 10:5,8–9 and states that with regard to a biblical framework of prayer evangelism, 'the most complete model is found in this passage':

> When you enter a house, first say, 'Peace to this house.' . . .
>
> When you enter a town and are welcomed, eat what is set before you. Heal the sick who are there and tell them, 'The kingdom of God is near you' (NIV).

Silvoso argues that Christ commands us to do four things for the lost:

1. Speak peace to them.
2. Fellowship with them.
3. Take care of their needs.
4. Proclaim the good news.

- He states that after discerning *who* is to be prayed for, the first step is blessing them in prayer. This is not just that *they* may receive the ultimate blessing of Christ, but that in doing so, God might change *our* heart towards them and give us an authentic love for them.
- The next step is deepening relationship with them – cultivating a genuine and uncontrived friendship in which we can demonstrate the difference Christ has made in our lives.
- The third step is to seek to meet their needs by praying specifically for them as well as being prepared to be the practical answer to those prayers.
- The final step is speaking to them about Christ and inviting them to church.

The impressive thing in Silvoso's model is that it is *incarnational*. Prayer for the lost is not seen in a vacuum.

Bill Hybels, in his book *Becoming a Contagious Christian*,[7] sets out the following missional formula:

> High Potency + Close Proximity + Clear Communication = Maximum Impact.

Living lives of spiritual power will not affect the lost unless we are living *with them* and able to *communicate* the reason for the hope we have when they ask us (as they surely will if our lives are characterized by authentic spiritual power).

Silvoso realizes this, and his model is holistic and involves cultivating relationship so that truth can be demonstrated. Many of us react against such an idea, but this is not a call to make artificial relationships with an evangelistic motive, but rather to commit to investing in a few existing relationships in a world in which many of us spread ourselves too thinly and take superficiality to new depths!

The other idea Silvoso raises is that of using prayer evangelistically to pray for the needs of our non-Christian friends. He encourages us to find out the needs of the people we are interceding for and not only pray for them but *tell them* we are praying for them, so that answered prayer can be evangelistic.

Many of us would shy away from this, but I can remember the time I discovered its value inadvertently. After my curacy I was chaplain of a Young Offenders prison near Bristol. Each Sunday morning I took the chapel service, which was a short service of worship, testimony and teaching. Like most Anglican churches, we often had a time for intercession, and I would get prayer requests from the guys. I would then publicly pray for them, which they were always really grateful for. This had only happened a few times when a guy came to me and said that he now really believed, because 'God has answered the prayer.' This led to the young man giving his life to Christ. This caught me off guard because I was simply doing the intercessions and didn't expect God to answer!

George Müller (1805–98) was in the habit of praying for the salvation of his non-Christian friends in the way we have discussed. He began praying for *five* of his friends. He prayed five years before the first one was converted. For the next one he prayed ten years; for the third one, twenty-five years; and for the fourth one, just under fifty years. He sadly died before the last one was converted – on 10 March 1898, after fifty-two years of prayer – at Müller's funeral.

The power of prayer

> So the word of God spread. The number of disciples in Jerusalem increased rapidly, and a large number of priests became obedient to the faith.

The early church knew about the power of prayer. On the day of Pentecost the church was born and Acts 2:41 records that 3,000 were converted after Peter's sermon. Things are not what they were: 1 sermon = 3,000 converted; today we have *3,000 sermons* and rejoice if we see *1 person* converted! Prayer is evangelistically powerful!

When I was a curate I went to Kenya to visit one of our church's mission partners working in a town called Kitui. There I met a remarkable man by the name of George Kataeki Tuisme. Pastor George had been powerfully converted in prison and had an unusual ministry of evangelism that was accompanied by healing and other signs and wonders. On a later visit to my parish in

England he prophesied (to the concern of the elders!) that a woman in our church who was very ill with chronic multiple sclerosis was going to be healed, *but not yet*. At a meeting some weeks later George and the elders prayed for the woman and she was instantly healed. From being in a wheelchair, she danced up and down the chancel steps, was horse-riding the following week and is now in full-time evangelistic ministry. As well as an unusual ministry, George also had an unusual prayer life – he prayed for hours on end, getting up before sunrise and taking himself off for extended periods of solitude. Unusual ministry, unusual prayer life – I wondered to myself if there was a connection? I asked Pastor George to teach me about prayer. His teaching was profound in its simplicity:

> Do you want to know how to learn to pray? *Pray!* . . . the anointing of grace you have demands action. *Prayer* is the action . . . the greater anointing depends on prayer. As you pray, so the anointing comes . . . five minutes' prayer – five minutes' anointing; sixty minutes' prayer – sixty minutes' anointing.

This concurs with the view of David Yonggi Cho, Senior Pastor of the world's largest church (the 830,000-strong Yoido Full Gospel Church in South Korea). He states, 'Little prayer, little power. Much prayer, much power.'

In Acts 6:7 I love the line: 'a large number of priests became obedient to the faith'. It's always great when the clergy get converted – a great asset to the furtherance of the kingdom, I always think! I am writing this from my house in Cornwall. Not far from here there was a famous clergy conversion. The Revd William Haslam (1818–1905) was a high church Anglican vicar who was converted by his own sermon. Haslam was Vicar of Baldhu near Truro and was very concerned when one of his servants got saved. After a period of being deeply convicted of his sin, Haslam himself was converted in 1851. I'll allow Haslam to speak for himself in the words of his autobiography, *From Death to Life*:

> I do not remember all I said, but I felt a wonderful light and joy coming into my soul, and I was beginning to see what the Pharisees did not. Whether it was in my words, or my manner, or my look, I know not; but all of a sudden, a local preacher, who happened to be in the congregation, stood up, and putting up his arms, shouted out in Cornish fashion, 'The parson is converted! The parson is converted! Hallelujah!' In another moment his voice was lost in the shouts and praises of three or four hundred of the congregation. Instead of rebuking this extraordinary 'brawling' as I should have done in former time, I joined in the outbreak of praise, and then gave out the Doxology – 'Praise God from whom all blessings flow', and the people sang it over and over again.
>
> At least twenty other people that morning found real peace through the Saviour. The news spread in all directions that 'the parson had been converted, and that in his own pulpit, and by his own sermon'.[8]

Shortly after his conversion William Haslam was visited by the infamous Billy Bray (1794–1868) – a local tin miner who was a fiery preacher and evangelist. Bray was so over the moon at the vicar's conversion that he picked him up and carried him around the dining-room for joy! Bray later explained to Haslam that he was so delighted because he had been praying for everyone on Baldhu Hill, on which the church was situated, since some years earlier when God had told him to intercede for the residents of that hill, and everyone would be saved.

It is amazing how often when someone comes to Christ, seemingly from nowhere, it turns out that someone has been praying for them. Jonathan Goforth (1859–1936) became the foremost missionary revivalist in early twentieth-century China. He experienced a remarkable working of the Holy Spirit in Manchuria (North-east China) during 1909 when multitudes came to Christ. The secret? Someone was praying! Goforth visited London during that same year. He was taken to a crippled woman who had an amazing ministry of intercession. During the conversation she asked Goforth to take a look at her notebook. She had noted three particular days during which she had had a special burden to pray for his meetings. Goforth was overwhelmed when he realized that they were the exact three days of the outpouring of the Holy Spirit in Manchuria.

How many times does this happen when a person does not get to see the fruit of their prayer?

When I was a lecturer at the London School of Theology, I took a group of students into HMP Feltham (the largest Young Offenders prison in Europe) on a weekly basis to run an Alpha course. During the week on prayer I played a clip from a video called *Transformations*, which chronicled a move of God in Cali, Colombia. The video explained that the situation there was really bad, with drug trafficking out of control and spiralling. In the midst of this very difficult situation the churches were divided and not working together. This situation changed when a local pastor was killed accidentally by the drug traffickers – he was caught in the crossfire. This tragedy caused the churches to start meeting together, which culminated in all-night prayer meetings in the city's vast football stadium. As thousands of Christians met together to intercede against the drug trade and the ills of the city, things began to change. Many of the drug barons were caught and imprisoned, the murder rate fell and crime went down. Even the civic authorities made a connection between this positive change and the nights of prayer, and they even gave the use of the stadium to the churches rent-free.

After the video I could see a young man to my left in floods of tears – very unusual in the tough context of a prison. After the talk there was an opportunity for people to come forward for prayer, but he stayed in his seat until it was time for him to be escorted back to his cell.

The following week, as soon as the talk was over, he was the first up for prayer, explaining that he wanted to become a Christian. His name was Carlos and he was from Cali, Columbia. He was in prison for smuggling drugs into prison. He explained to me that the previous week he had been too upset to come forward. He said when he saw the bit in the video when the pastor died, 'I felt I had done it – as if my fingers were on the trigger.' He had gone back to his cell and had not been able to get this out of his head all week and had been crying, not even able to sleep.

This was the strongest case of the Holy Spirit convicting a person of sin that I have ever seen. When I reflected on what had happened, it didn't take long for me to realize that it was the *prayers* of all those praying saints that had effected this miracle. If only they knew that their sacrificial nocturnal intercession not only changed the climate of their city – but over 5,000 miles away would bring a Cali teenager to Christ in a London prison!

Prayer works! Prayer is powerful! Prayer is vital to evangelism! After the ascension of Christ, the first disciples did not begin the great commission but, out of obedience to Jesus, simply waited. They began by returning to Jerusalem – to the Upper Room where once Christ had shared his Last Supper with them – and in that place they devoted themselves to prayer. Shortly after this, the power of God fell on them and they began to turn the ancient world upside down. Historians still muse over how this crestfallen and persecuted sect of Judaism could morph into the world's largest religion, claiming the allegiance of a third of the population of the planet.

But first . . . they had to receive God's power, and for that they got on their knees. This is the key! We can only be effective witnesses once the risen Christ has empowered us. Our prayers are a vehicle for his power.

Let us repent of our lukewarmness and pledge to become a people of prayer.

> Lord Jesus, clothe me with power from on high so that I might become a contagious witness for you, in [*your town*], in [*your county*], and even to the very ends of the earth!

Postscript

Not Converts But Disciples
Evangelism and follow-up

Andy Economides

> The temper of our times is for instant gratification and short-term commitment – quick answers to prayer and quick results with a minimum of effort and discomfort. There is no such thing as easy and instant discipleship. One can commence a walk of discipleship in a moment, but the first step must lengthen into a life-long walk.
>
> William Carey,
> pioneer missionary to India (1761–1834)[1]

During my college days in London I studied engineering. At the college I befriended a fellow student and told him how Christ had transformed my life. After five months I carefully presented this student (who was called J.John) with a book about Jesus.

A few days later J.John said to me, 'I read the book and prayed the prayer. What do I do now?' He had accepted Jesus Christ's invitation and decided to open the door of his life to Christ (Rev. 3:20). That very week I introduced him to the church youth fellowship and to my Christian friends.

I discipled him for the next two years. J.John soon became a mature disciple and today is one of the most effective communicators of the Christian faith in the world.

We have an obligation to follow up. It is a privilege but also a joy to do so.

Jesus Christ's famous last words to his disciples were:

> Therefore go and make *disciples* of all nations, baptizing them in the name of the Father and of the Son and of the Holy Spirit, and teaching them to obey everything I have commanded you. And surely I am with you always, to the very end of the age.
>
> Matthew 28:19–20 NIV

We call this the Great Commission. Notice that Jesus did not say to go and just make *converts* but *disciples*. To make disciples it is first necessary to follow up those who accept the call to live for Christ. During Jesus' life the twelve apostles and many other followers were seen as his 'disciples', which means 'pupils' or 'apprentices'.

Akolouthein is the common and normal Greek verb that means to 'follow'. It is used of the disciples who left their various trades and occupations and followed Jesus (Mark 1:18). It is the word that Jesus used to summon people to himself. On Jesus' lips it is the word of challenge. His commandment to Matthew is: '*Follow* me' (Mark 2:14 NIV).

One day, Jesus called his disciples and the people around him and said to them, 'If anyone would come after me, he must deny himself and take up his cross and follow me' (Mark 8:34 NIV).

The disciple is the learner and the listener who must listen to the words of Jesus and who must follow their thread, so that day by day he or she may learn more of the wisdom that Jesus is ever willing to teach. This wisdom gives life for the follower. This wisdom, when followed, makes a difference in and through the believer.

The marks of maturity

Looking at the New Testament, we can say there are at least five hallmarks of a believer who has reached maturity in Christ.

1. Assured

A mature disciple is someone who has the *assurance* of salvation, which is the assurance of eternal life (1 John 5:13). This person is someone who knows the Father, through Christ and in the power of the Holy Spirit. They know God personally. A disciple follows the ways of Christ because Jesus is Lord. To all who receive and believe in Christ, to them alone God gives the right to become his children. They are born of God. This is not a physical birth resulting from human passion or plan; this birth comes from God (John 1:12–13). All believers have this. Mature believers *know* this.

2. Spirit-filled

A mature disciple is someone who is continually empowered by the Holy Spirit. The apostle Paul, writing to the Christians at Ephesus, urges them to be filled with the Holy Spirit. Obviously these Christians were already indwelt by the Holy Spirit, so what was Paul meaning? 'Be filled with the Holy Spirit' in the original Greek text meant being continually filled. Jesus Christ told his disciples that when the Holy Spirit came upon them, they would receive power to be his witnesses (Acts 1:8). We will return to this later, as the fullness of the Holy Spirit is not just a hallmark of maturity but the chief means to attaining maturity.

3. Christ-like

A mature disciple is someone who is like Christ. To be like the Master is to be sanctified – made holy.

This is very practical and should find a very obvious expression in our dealings with others. Our attitude towards others should be the same as Jesus'. Disciples should not only look at their own interests, but to the interests of others. The challenge for the disciple is to learn to see things from the other's point of view. This will lead to a practical demonstration of love. Disciples can love others when they allow God's word to dwell in their hearts. Our attitude can change if we let the Lord, by his Spirit, transform our inner being.

4. Serving others

All Christians have gifts. The mature Christian *knows* his gifts and puts them to work in the service of *others*.

Paul employs a biological metaphor to explain how this works. The human body has many parts, but the many parts make up one body. So it is with the church, the body of Christ. There are many individual disciples and they make up the church. Everyone in the church has a unique purpose. God has gifts to give to each Christian for the *common good* – not individual blessing. In Romans 12:5–8, Paul writes:

> so in Christ we who are many form one body, and each member belongs to all the others. We have different gifts,

> according to the grace given us. If a man's gift is prophesying, let him use it in proportion to his faith. If it is serving, let him serve; if it is teaching, let him teach; if it is encouraging, let him encourage; if it is contributing to the needs of others, let him give generously; if it is leadership, let him govern diligently; if it is showing mercy, let him do it cheerfully (NIV).

Every Christian has at least one of these *ministry* gifts of grace listed in chapter 12 of Romans.

Another set of gifts are *spiritual gifts*, mentioned by Paul in 1 Corinthians 12:8–10. We can experience one or more of these gifts of the Holy Spirit occasionally or regularly as he wills and we desire. To desire these gifts is essential to receiving them, as this is an expression of faith. The gifts of the Holy Spirit mentioned here are wisdom, knowledge, faith, healing, miracles, prophecy, discernment of spirits, tongues and the interpretation of tongues.

Another set of gifts are *offices* that Christ gives to the church by calling individual believers to these positions. Christ makes some apostles, some prophets, some evangelists, some pastors and some teachers. Their responsibility is to equip God's people for works of service so that the body of Christ may be built up. This will lead to unity in our faith, to knowing God's Son and to maturity, becoming increasingly Christ-like (Eph. 4:11–13).

5. A spiritual parent

> I write to you, dear children, because your sins have been forgiven on account of his name.
>
> I write to you, fathers, because you have known him who is from the beginning.

> I write to you, young men, because you have overcome the evil one.
>
> 1 John 2:12–13 NIV

John clearly sees a progression in the Christian life from being a child to being an adolescent and then a parent. Another name for a child is a *dependant* – they lack maturity to take responsibility for others. A parent, however, has to have the maturity to act selflessly and take responsibility for others.

Take a look at a mature disciple and you will see someone who has moved beyond being concerned with only their own spiritual life and can take responsibility for others in the body of Christ. They have become a spiritual father or mother – not simply experiencing forgiveness or even victory over sin but having such a knowledge of God that they are able to disciple others.

The means to maturity

We have explored five marks of maturity – but how do we arrive there? We will now look at five means to attaining maturity. If the believer is to become a mature follower of Christ, he will need to be . . .

1. Committed to the church

A few weeks after I became a follower of Christ at the age of 17, a contemporary named Andrew Liversidge came to my home. I knew him slightly from school days. He had heard that I had become a committed follower of Jesus Christ and asked if I would like to join the church youth fellowship that he attended. I am so glad that he cared enough to follow up my decision to follow Christ.

I started to attend the youth fellowship, which met on Saturday and Sunday evenings. Soon I also went to the Wednesday evening meeting, which met in the youth leader's home for Bible study, prayer and fellowship. The youth leader, Roger Stacey, became a spiritual father to me. Those early years were vital in my formation and development as a disciple. The love and care that Roger and his wife Kate gave to me was wonderful. They were true shepherds. Later I became one of the leaders of the youth fellowship. It was there that I met a lovely young woman whom I fell in love with and married! During this time I also attended church regularly on Sunday mornings and became friends with other Christians.

Disciples need to be part of a community of believers – that is, the church. It is worth noting that contrary to common usage, throughout the New Testament the word 'church' is never used to describe a building. It always describes a community of people who have given their hearts to God. In fact the Greek word *ekklesia*, which is translated 'church', literally means 'gathering' or 'community'.

This fellowship is the coming together of people in friendship. In the early church those who heard, believed and accepted the message of Christ spent their time learning from the apostles' teachings, taking part in the fellowship, and sharing in the fellowship meals and the prayers (Acts 2:42). The church is the community of believers in togetherness and friendship.

The early church continued together in close fellowship and even shared their belongings with one another. They would sell property and possessions and give the money to the apostles to distribute among those in the church who were in need (Acts 2:44). The church should be a sharing community of people who demonstrate practical love for one another.

2. Grounded in the Bible

Christians attain maturity by hearing and receiving God's word. We receive God's word as we draw teaching from the Bible, church meetings (in the form of a sermon) and other Christians on a one-to-one basis.

It is a big advantage to have a healthy and positive attitude when we hear the word of God taught. Make a decision to take home at least a crumb from every meeting. Read, reflect on and apply the word. Discipline yourself to set aside time to do this.

New disciples benefit greatly from reading and reflecting on the accounts of Jesus found in the Gospels. Start by reading Mark's Gospel straight through in just a few sittings. Then go back to the beginning and read a small section at a time. Think and reflect. Take your time. Enjoy it. Let it touch your heart. Let it speak. Spend months on this Gospel. Ask yourself after each small section, 'What did Jesus say? What did he do?' Look at his compassion. Is there a promise to claim? Is there a sin to repent of? Is there an encouragement to take? Allow him to speak to you. By doing this you will certainly get to know him more.

3. Persistent in prayer

There is power in prayer. We will never attain maturity in Christ if we neglect prayer. Seven days without prayer makes one weak. No wonder the theologian L. A. T. Van Doren referred to prayer as 'the Christian's vital breath'.

The early church devoted themselves to prayer and praise in public places and in their homes (Acts 2:42–47). Prayer is simply speaking and listening to God. Prayer includes praise, thanksgiving and biblical meditation (reading and thinking about the word of God).

God is holy and we are not, so prayer includes confession of sin. God is our heavenly Father once we have believed in Jesus and received him into our lives (John 1:12–13). We can tell him about our needs and ask for his help. Prayer also includes praying for others – intercession. God loves the world and so must we. Often we are prompted as we pray to help in practical ways.

4. Taking the sacraments seriously

There are two sacraments instituted by Christ – Baptism and the Lord's Supper (also called the Communion or Eucharist). A sacrament has been defined as an outward and visible sign of an inward and spiritual grace. When we receive them in faith, they are a means of grace – a means to maturity in Christ. Given this, it is remarkable that some Christians do not take them seriously. There are even some Christian churches where they are not practised.

Baptism is the sacrament of Christian initiation. Whoever knows Christ as their Saviour and Lord should be baptized. There are three good reasons for baptism. First, we should be baptized in *obedience* to Jesus Christ. Jesus gave the Great Commission to the church, instructing them to baptize disciples in the name of the Father, the Son and the Holy Spirit (Matt. 28:18–20).

Second, baptism is to *prepare* us to serve Christ. Jesus' baptism prepared him to serve God and others. At the moment Jesus came up out of the water, he saw the Spirit of God descending in the form of a dove and a voice said, 'This is my Son, whom I love; with him I am well pleased' (Matt. 3:17 NIV). After this experience Jesus went out to preach and heal.

The third reason for baptism is to *demonstrate* our faith in Christ. The person being baptized is identifying himself or herself as a Christian. The act shows that the person is not ashamed of who they are and their decision to follow Jesus Christ (Mark 8:38).

What is the meaning of baptism? There are four meanings. First, baptism signifies the washing away of sins. Just as water cleanses our bodies, so baptism is a sign that our sins have been washed away from us.

Second, baptism demonstrates the burying of our old life. During baptism the immersing under the water represents what happens when someone dies and is buried in the ground. Baptism represents death of the person's old life and ways (Rom. 6:4). The old life has gone. When the person is raised from the water, it represents new life. Becoming a Christian is about becoming a new creation; the old has gone and the new has come, and all this is from God (2 Cor. 5:17).

Third, baptism is a sign of our receiving the Holy Spirit. Peter told the crowd to turn from sin and be baptized, and they would receive the Holy Spirit. Jesus and Paul received the Holy Spirit with power at baptism. Expect to receive God's power at baptism. Baptism in water and baptism in the Holy Spirit are sometimes linked in experience, and this shows itself in Scripture (1 Cor. 12:12–13).

Fourth, baptism is a sign that we have joined the church, the body of Christ. By baptism we are brought into the family of the church. All Christians, whatever nationality and background, should be baptized. The word 'baptism' means to immerse, plunge or sink. This is why many churches baptize people by completely immersing them in water. Baptism was done this way in New Testament times and Jesus was baptized this way in the River Jordan. Today, people can be baptized in a church building, a river, the sea, a swimming pool – in fact anywhere where there is water. Have you been baptized? If not, what is keeping you from being baptized? What are you waiting for? Ask your church leaders to baptize you!

Communion is the sacrament of Christian discipleship. It is a tangible sign from God to us that he has covenanted to save us – the seal of that promise being the blood of his Son shed on the cross two thousand years ago. In Communion we look back to remember that, but we also look forward to when Christ will return at the end of history for his church. For the Christian, it is the public sign that the believer is continuing to trust Christ and follow him.

The origin of this sacrament is in the fellowship meals of the early church, when the believers would come together to eat and drink, with an opportunity to remember the death of Christ with bread and wine representing his body and blood. Over the centuries it evolved out of a meal and became integrated in a service without the meal and just using the bread and wine, as we have it today.

Receiving Communion regularly means we never forget the cross. As we break bread with the community of faith, God will deepen our faith and draw us back to the place of intimacy with himself.

5. Baptized with the Holy Spirit

The Holy Spirit is not just the object of our worship (as God) but also the chief means by which we attain maturity in the faith. Put simply, *it takes God to know God*, and the thing that sets Christianity apart from every other religion is that God provides *himself* as a means of knowing himself!

The Bible tells us that the Holy Spirit is a counsellor, comforter and divine helper. Jesus Christ promised his disciples that they would experience a *baptism* with the Holy Spirit. Jesus told them that he was going away, back to God, but that he would give them the Holy Spirit. Jesus always addressed the Holy Spirit in the personal pronoun ('him' or 'he'), never the impersonal ('it') (John 14:15–17; 16:5–11).

The Lord's desire and plan is for disciples to be baptized in the Holy Spirit; that is, to be *completely immersed in the Holy Spirit*. Jesus is the baptizer (John 1:33). So how do we receive the fullness of God's Spirit? I want to suggest three steps:

First, confess any sin in our lives. The *Holy* Spirit is the Holy Spirit. He will not remain in power in a sinful life. He is sensitive. Heavenly waters will not flow through polluted channels. So it is necessary for disciples to take the first step and confess and turn away from any wrongdoing. We see that in the early church the Holy Spirit was given to those who obeyed him (Acts 5:32).

Second, we must simply *ask*. Jesus said the Holy Spirit is given easily to those who simply ask (Luke 11:13). Jesus described the Holy Spirit to the woman at the well as living water and invited her to ask for this gift of God (John 4:10). Have you ever asked God for the fullness of his Spirit?

The third step is to *believe* in Christ's promise when he says, regarding the Holy Spirit: 'If anyone is thirsty, let him come to me and drink. Whoever believes in me, as the Scripture has said, streams of living water will flow from within him' (John 7:37–38 NIV).

Since the fullness of the Spirit is a promise from Jesus, begging and pleading is not required and can even be a hindrance, as it does not come from faith. Faith involves gratefully *receiving*. It is a gift – take it. You do not need to persuade Jesus to be kind to you and baptize you with his Holy Spirit and fire. He has already promised.

Come with boldness to collect what he offers you. It is a gift, so you must believe the Giver, before you reach out to receive what he offers you. God offers his Holy Spirit to all. On the day of Pentecost Peter said, 'The promise is for you and your children and for all who are far off – for all whom the Lord our God will call' (Acts 2:39 NIV).

For many people the baptism with the Holy Spirit comes after becoming a Christian (Acts 8:15–16; 19:1–7). For some, conversion and the baptism in the Holy Spirit happen at the same time. You need not wait for a special service or preacher – you can ask and believe now. Find a place where you can pray, or ask a Christian friend to help you to pray a prayer like this:

> Lord Jesus,
> I thank you for dying on the cross for me.
> I surrender my life totally to you today.
> I ask you to forgive my sin . . . [*mention particular things*].
> I renounce completely my involvement in . . . [*let the Holy Spirit bring things to mind*].
> I ask you now to give me your promised gift and baptize me with your Holy Spirit.
> Jesus, baptizer in the Holy Spirit, immerse me in the life of your Spirit.
> I receive you now, Holy Spirit.
> Come, Holy Spirit . . . [*pause and focus on the Lord*].
> In the name of Jesus Christ.
> Amen.

If you have asked and believed, God will keep his promise. We only receive baptism in the Holy Spirit once, for all time. However, we need to ask God to fill us with his Holy Spirit over and over again, every day, as we face certain situations and tasks.

The formula is simple: *one baptism, many fillings, constant anointing.*

May the Lord bless you as you seek maturity in him.

May he assist you as you seek to be a person of the word, prayer and the sacraments, living it out in the community of his church and in the world, by the fullness of his Spirit.

Endnotes

Chapter 1: How to Communicate Effectively

[1] Carried out by the Philo Trust in 2000.

Chapter 2: A Picture is Worth a Thousand Words

[1] Interview in *Diva* magazine, http://www.divainternational.ch/spip.php?article113

Chapter 3: This is My Story

[1] Amazon review by Sofia, Bristol, UK, 26 March 2008. *Dreams from my Father* published by Canongate Books.

Chapter 4: Divine Comedy

[1] Gerry Maguire Thompson, *Positive Comedy Training*, www.positivecomedy.com

Chapter 5: All Roads Lead to God

[1] Michael Haykin, *Defence of the Truth: Contending for the faith yesterday and today* (Darlington: Evangelical Press, 2004), p. 8.

[2] Hans Kung, *Does God Exist? An Answer for Today* (New York: Doubleday, 1980), p. 587.

[3] Karen Armstrong, *The Battle for God: Fundamentalism in Judaism, Christianity and Islam* (London: HarperCollins, 2001), p. xiii.

[4] Armstrong, *The Battle for God*, p. xiii.

[5] Armstrong, *The Battle for God*, p. xiv.

[6] Vinoth Ramachandra, *Faiths in Conflict: Christian Integrity in a Multi-Cultural World* (Nottingham: Inter-Varsity Press, 1999), p. 127.

[7] The ancient Greeks, following Plato, often separated their understanding of reality into the realm of mind, idea or spirit and the material and physical. The realm of mind and idea was good and superior; the physical realm was considered inferior or even evil. Consequently, the idea that God would want to raise a physical corpse from death seemed absurd to them.

[8] John Hick, *God Has Many Names* (Philadelphia: Westminster, 1982), p. 58.

[9] Kung, *Does God Exist?*, p. 607.

[10] Ajith Fernando, 'The Uniqueness of Jesus Christ', in *Telling the Truth: Evangelizing Postmoderns*, ed. D. A. Carson (Grand Rapids: Zondervan, 2000), p. 124.

[11] Ronald H. Nash, *Is Jesus the Only Savior?* (Grand Rapids: Zondervan, 1994), p. 10.

[12] Nash, *Is Jesus the Only Savior?*, p. 24 (footnote 22).

[13] Samir Selmanovic, 'The Sweet Problem of Inclusiveness: Facing Our God in the Other', in *An Emergent Manifesto of Hope*, ed. Doug Pagitt and Tony Jones (Grand Rapids: Baker Books, 2007), p. 192.

[14] Selmanovic, 'The Sweet Problem', p. 192.

[15] Selmanovic, 'The Sweet Problem', p. 192.
[16] Nash, *Is Jesus the Only Savior?*, p. 11.
[17] Greg L. Bahnsen, *Always Ready: Directions for defending the Faith* (Nacogdoches: Covenant Media Press, 1996), p. 241.
[18] Bahnsen, *Always Ready*, p. 243.
[19] Bahnsen, *Always Ready*, p. 244.
[20] F. F. Bruce, *The Book of the Acts: The New International Commentary on the New Testament* (Grand Rapids: Eerdmans, 1988), p. 203.
[21] Bruce, *Acts*, p. 210.
[22] Bahnsen, *Always Ready*, p. 241.
[23] Ramachandra, *Faiths in Conflict*, p. 135.
[24] Alister McGrath, *Bridge-Building: Effective Christian Apologetics* (Ebbw Vale: Inter-Varsity Press, 1992), p. 49.
[25] D. A. Carson, *The Gagging of God: Christianity Confronts Pluralism* (Leicester: Apollos, 1996), p. 497.
[26] Bahnsen, *Always Ready*, p. 246.
[27] Bahnsen, *Always Ready*, p. 248.
[28] Kung, *Does God Exist?*, p. 523.
[29] Bruce, *Acts*, p. 329.
[30] Bruce, *Acts*, p. 334.
[31] McGrath, *Bridge-Building*, p. 49.
[32] McGrath, it seems, is trying to read in a natural theology here to support the Thomistic nature–grace separation of classical apologetics and salvage a point of contact.
[33] Bahnsen, *Always Ready*, p. 256.
[34] Bruce, *Acts*, p. 335.
[35] Bahnsen, *Always Ready*, p. 260.
[36] Bruce, *Acts*, p. 339.
[37] Bahnsen, *Always Ready*, p. 261.
[38] F. F. Bruce, 'Paul and the Athenians', *The Expository Times*, Vol. 88 (October, 1976), p. 11.
[39] Bruce, *Acts*, p. 340.
[40] Bruce, *Acts*, p. 341.
[41] Bahnsen, *Always Ready*, p. 272.

[42] Bruce, *Acts*, p. 211.
[43] J. Andrew Kirk, *What is Mission?* (Minneapolis: Augsburg Fortress, 2000), p. 131.
[44] Nash, *Is Jesus the Only Savior?*, p. 139.
[45] Clark Pinnock, *A Wideness in God's Mercy* (Grand Rapids: Zondervan, 1992), p. 165.
[46] Pinnock, *A Wideness in God's Mercy*, p. 96.
[47] Nash, *Is Jesus the Only Savior?*, p. 170.
[48] Ramachandra, *Faiths in Conflict*, p. 167.

Chapter 7: How to People-Fish

[1] William Temple (1881–1944), quoted by Tony Cooke at www.tonycooke.org
[2] Rebecca Manley Pippert, *Out of the Saltshaker and Into the World* (Nottingham: Inter-Varsity Press, 1999).
[3] J. I. Packer in the Foreword to *The Gospel According to Jesus* by John MacArthur (Grand Rapids: Zondervan, 1988), p. ix.
[4] Charles G. Finney, 'How to Win Souls', published in *The Independent of New York*, 2 November 1871, p. 22.

Chapter 8: Singing the Song of Salvation

[1] Jim Firth, 'Speaking the Language of the Unchurched', quoted in Sally Morgenthaler, *Worship Evangelism: Inviting Unbelievers Into the Presence of God* (Grand Rapids: Zondervan, 1999).

Chapter 9: The Best Boat to Fish From

[1] Michael Green, *Evangelism through the Local Church* (London: Hodder & Stoughton, 1990), p. 408.

Chapter 10: Demonstrating the Good News

1 Lausanne Committee for World Evangelization, *Evangelism and Social Responsibility*, ed. John Stott (New York: World Evangelical Fellowship, 1982).

2 Victor Hugo, *Les Miserables* (London: Penguin Classics, 1980).

3 William Wilberforce, *A Practical view of the prevailing religious system of professed Christians* (1835).

4 William Wilberforce's abolition speech, delivered in the House of Commons on Tuesday, 12 May 1789, from 'William Wilberforce's Sentimental Rhetoric: Parliamentary Reportage and the Abolition Speech of 1789' in *The Age of Johnson: A Scholarly Annual*, 14 (2003), pp. 281–305.

5 *The Lausanne Covenant* (Lausanne Committee for World Evangelization, 1974).

6 *The Lausanne Covenant*.

7 John Stott, *Christian Mission in the Modern World* (Nottingham: Inter-Varsity Press, 1974).

8 Stott, *Christian Mission in the Modern World*.

9 Stott, *Christian Mission in the Modern World*.

10 Vinoth Ramachandra (2006), available at www.micahnetwork.org

11 Tim Keller, *Ministries of Mercy: The Call of the Jericho Road* (Phillipsburg, NJ: P&R Publishing, 2nd edition, 1997).

12 Keller, *Ministries of Mercy*.

13 Keller, *Ministries of Mercy*.

14 Lausanne Committee for World Evangelization, *Evangelism and Social Responsibility*.

15 Lausanne Committee for World Evangelization, *Evangelism and Social Responsibility*.

16 Lausanne Committee for World Evangelization, *Evangelism and Social Responsibility*.

[17] The earliest reference to this quotation comes from 1873, in an essay by Robert G. Ingersoll.

[18] Matthew Parris, *The Times*, 27 December 2008.

Chapter 11: Ministering in the Miraculous

[1] C. S. Lewis, 'Miracles' in *God in the Dock: Essays on Theology and Ethics*, ed. Walter Hooper (Grand Rapids: Eerdmans), pp. 29–30.

Chapter 12: Preaching the Full Gospel

[1] A. B. Simpson, *The Gospel of Healing* (Camp Hill, PA: WingSpread Publishers, 1986).

[2] Richard Fletcher, *The Conversion of Europe* (London: Harper Collins, 1997), p. 62.

Chapter 13: Take the Roof Off Your Thinking!

[1] From www.brainyquote.com

Chapter 14: Breaking Out from the Four Walls of the Church

[1] *The Lausanne Covenant* (Lausanne Committee for World Evangelization, 1974).

Chapter 15: Out of Africa

[1] From the online dictionary ardictionary.com

[2] Vinay Samuel and Chris Sugden, *Mission as Transformation: A Theology of the Whole Gospel* (Milton Keynes: Paternoster, 2000).

Chapter 16: God the Evangelist

[1] R. A. Torrey, *The Place of Prayer in Evangelism* (1907).

[2] Lausanne Committee for World Evangelization, *Evangelism and Social Responsibility*, ed. John Stott (World Evangelical Fellowship, 1982).

[3] 'Prayer in Evangelism', Lausanne Occasional Paper No. 42 (Forum for World Evangelization, 2004).

[4] 8 December 1997.

[5] Torrey, *The Place of Prayer in Evangelism*.

[6] Ed Silvoso, *Prayer Evangelism* (Ventura, CA: Regal, 2000).

[7] Bill Hybels, *Becoming a Contagious Christian* (Grand Rapids: Zondervan, 1996).

[8] William Haslam, *From Death to Life* (Charleston, SC: Biblio Bazaar, 2007).

Postscript: Not Converts But Disciples

[1] From *The Baptist Page*, www.baptistpage.com